An Update from the Author

This book was written in 1997 and updated again in 2000 for publication through a self-publisher. The book as published in paperback had thirty-three chapters, but some of those were fillers and fluff, having little to do with relationship issues and nothing to do with John Gray.

In this 2011-updated version for electronic publication and 2012 re-release in paperback, I eliminated six chapters and several illustrations that encompassed outdated events or people no longer in the spotlight. Only minor editing corrections and sporadic updates were made from the original manuscript.

If a woman does not agree with John Gray's one-size-fits-all fundamentalist approach to male-female relationships, or if a woman ever had a relationship that ended poorly with a man, such a woman will appreciate the humor in this book. Men can still appreciate the writing and lessons herein, because successful relationships are built on mutual understanding and trust, and plenty of men do not fit John Gray's selfish and detached prototype of the typical male.

Men are from Mars, Women are from Venus was misogynistic claptrap that should have been published as a pamphlet, and not spawned at least ten different Mars/Venus books on relationships since 1992. To be blunt, I destroy John Gray's authoritarian approach to relationships through the heavy but truthful application of sarcasm and humor.

Enjoy the laughs.

Introduction

The title of this book is a parody of John Gray's *Men are from Mars, Women are from Venus* (*A Practical Guide for Improving Communication and Getting What You Want in Your Relationships*). The 1990s produced a plethora of books about how well men and women can get along if they just understand each other. Please! We've had thousands of years to understand and adapt to each other...why do so many authors pretend to have the answer to relationships?

It makes more sense to me to accentuate a point through humor than psychological babble and philosophical nonsense. My book does not offer a quick fix or any deep answers to understanding the opposite sex or mending a troubled marriage. But I do dispute Dr. Gray's rudimentary opinions and believe that through humor and a somewhat realistic look at male/female relationships, I make the argument that John Gray is way off course.

All of Dr. Gray's books, regardless of their titles, run along concurrent lines and reiterate common themes. In addition to parodying *Men are from Mars, Women are from Venus*, I have included spin-off tidbits from *Mars and Venus Together Forever* (*Relationship Skills for Lasting Love*), which was formerly entitled *What Your Mother Couldn't Tell You and Your Father Didn't Know*, and *Mars and Venus in the Bedroom* (*A Guide to Lasting Romance and Passion*), which includes graphic and sexually explicit material and should have an NC-17 rating. It was impossible to parody each book separately because, as previously stated, all his books are virtually identical in nature.

I've found that many self-improvement and inspirational books are based on a clinical perspective of female/male relationships. While this may be helpful for an individual or a couple in a counseling environment, once you leave the session and reenter the real world having to deal with real problems, the lessons you learned are quickly forgotten. That's why counseling is not as effective as most psychologists claim it is.

Remove the psychologist from his clinical setting and see how he deals with a couple constantly fighting over the pettiest of issues. Instead of a quiet office, a desk, two plush leather chairs and a Tiffany lamp, put the doctor behind the wheel of a car stuck in rush hour traffic and see how he deals with the fighting couple. Suddenly his messages of deep breathing and calm, rational discussion are replaced with swearing and giving the bird to slow drivers. He'll need to write a prescription of Xanax for himself when he finally gets home to his own family.

My book is literally a celebration of liberation. I am not talking about women's lib, but rather a break from the monotony of self-reference guides that are supposed to liberate us from all our problems. A clinical perspective achieves its goal nearly 100% of the time when confined to a clinical environment. Change the environment and chaos continues to reign. This book dispels the myth that self-help books are the solution to life's ills. The key to developing relationships and preserving existing ones is the ability to laugh at each other and ourselves, while continually being mindful that no one is perfect and no one has all the answers.

I found John Gray's book *Men are from Mars, Women are from Venus* sexist and demeaning to women, and insulting to men. Dr. Gray's idea that women should be subservient to men's wishes and desires does not foster understanding, nor does it make for better marriages. Marital discord and dysfunctional families are the result of this type of thinking.

The underlying message to Dr. Gray's readers is that women need to settle for less, shut up, and pull back when men need time by themselves. This thought borders dangerously on both misogamy (hatred of marriage) and misogyny (hatred of women). Suggestions abound on how women could improve themselves, but very few on what men could do. His book, clearly aimed at a female audience, is patronizing and contemptuous.

Men are from Mars, Women are from Venus was one of the best selling books of the 1990s decade. Despite that fact, I have found overwhelming dislike for that book among my contemporaries! Why is this the case? In my view, beyond the clever, but decidedly overused, Martian-Venusian metaphor, lies the ugly specter of fundamentalism. Anyone who advocates the sentiment that fundamentalism is the answer to troubled relationships is asking for an antagonistic relationship at best and a divorce at worst.

I wrote *Women May Be From Venus, But Men Are Really From Uranus* because Dr. Gray's book insulted my intelligence and degraded the integrity and autonomy of every woman on this planet. Yes, I poke fun at the modern male, sometimes bordering on male bashing and vulgarity, but I did it in the true spirit of humor, not to be taken too seriously. Genuine enlightenment, regardless of the subject matter, comes when an individual confronts both sides of an issue and reaches a viable conclusion.

Therefore, it is my hope that the entertainment and observations in this book inspire us to take life as seriously as nature intends us to take it, which isn't that serious at all. We have to constantly remind ourselves just how small we are in the whole scheme of life in order to truly appreciate each other. Live and laugh *together*, *share* your warmth and your knowledge, *mutually* rise to face challenges, and strive to achieve *common* goals. That is the ultimate key to understanding each other and enjoying better relationships.

This book is my rebuttal of *Men are from Mars, Women are from Venus*, as well as his other books, as seen from a woman's point of view. In no way should this be considered a scientific rebuttal; this is merely a chance to laugh at Dr. Gray's one-dimensional opinion of relationships. I've done my best to address different perspectives that expose men as the less dominant sex in a paradoxical venue, and by the time you've finished reading this book, I think you'll agree that men are not from Mars...they're from Uranus.

TABLE OF CONTENTS

An Update from the Author
Introduction

SECTION ONE: BRACE YOURSELF, DR. GRAY, YOU'RE BEING REBUTTED

SECTION TWO: FROM BLACK TO GRAY: MY OTHER OBSERVATIONS

- 1 -
PLANET URANUS

So are men really from Mars? I don't think so. Granted, Martian fossils have been discovered that indicate life may once have existed there but this life form was very primitive with little possibility of advanced brain function. Hmm. On second thought, maybe there is something to this 'men from Mars thing' after all.

Men are complex creatures, driven by the thought from two heads. The little one usually wins and that must make the big one jealous. This is manifested in their personalities. Sometimes you get a dozen roses and sometimes you get nothing. The Little Head is responsible for the roses. It knows that in order to get what it needs to survive, it must pander to the female's weakness for flowers. The Little Head also invented chocolate. See the pattern? Men without independently thinking Little Heads usually go insane. No flowers, no chocolate; just concentration camps, gas chambers and machines of war. Pathetic, isn't it?

Planet Uranus (pronounced your-anus) is a large, gaseous planet, the seventh from our sun. This planet is best suited for men because it so aptly describes them. It's made up largely of gas and is very dense. Satellite imagery has revealed landscape best suited for horse and car racing, with ample crater space for fishing contests. Even Voyager, while circling Uranus, picked up an unmistakable radio signal that sounded like Lynyrd Skynyrd's 'Sweet Home Alabama.'

There has been some misconception about how to pronounce the planet's name. The correct pronunciation is above. But some television newscasters have another way of saying it. They pronounce it as urine-us or your-onus. Although this is completely wrong, you can't help but wonder what Tom Brokaw would look like if he had to announce to the world that scientists have just discovered rings around Uranus.

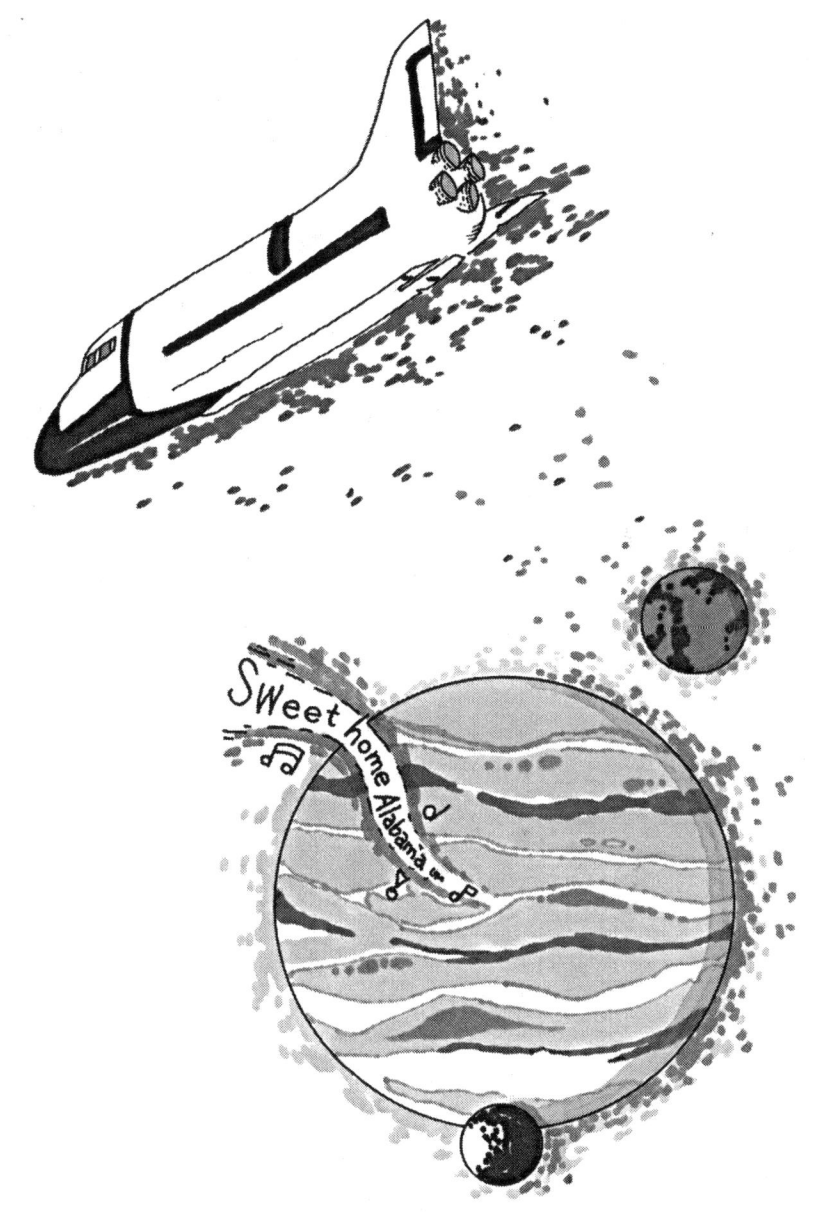

Should men ever decide to colonize Uranus, they are welcome to it. Men won't go to Mercury because that's the name of a car that just doesn't perform like a Ferrari. Venus belongs to women (at least I agree with John Gray on that point) because Venus is named after the goddess of love and beauty and what better way is there to describe women than that? For those who point out that Venus' clouds are composed of sulfuric and hydrochloric acid, perhaps they've never seen a woman's reaction to her tenth wedding anniversary without the customary diamond jewelry.

Mars is a candy bar. There's no way men will ever settle on something that brings to mind sweetness and sugary thoughts. Mars is also named after the god of war. Trying to get your husband to clear his dishes after a meal may seem like a war, but that hardly proves men came from that planet. Jupiter is a viable option for men. The trouble is that Jupiter doesn't seem to have any surface, so setting up a racetrack might prove difficult. Saturn, unfortunately, is the name of another car. Better than a Mercury but still not sporty or fast enough for men. Men might think of Saturn as somewhat homey as its rings are reminiscent of those in any bachelor's bathtub.

That leaves Uranus, Neptune and Pluto. Pluto is a Disney dog. And although the dog is man's best friend, don't believe that men will ever live on a dog. Live on the lamb and high off the hog, but not on the dog. Neptune, like Uranus, is a gas giant. While that might make it a close cousin of Uranus, Neptune is greenish in color. Grown men don't appreciate green. Look what they keep doing to the rain forests. Do they ever stop complaining about money? And when was the last time one of them didn't put up a fight when asked to mow the lawn?

Sorry, fellas. All that remains is Uranus.

- 2 -
IN THE BEGINNING...

..there was nothing. The world was awash in volcanic activity, sulfur clouds and the stench of a gaseous atmosphere. Kind of like Saturday night after bowling. Life was just beginning in a pool of water. Two separate organisms, having just formed themselves, came together, had a brief relationship, one kicked the other out of the pool and then promptly found another organism to shack up with. The one left in the pool was the male organism.

The other organism had to become independent. This was the female. You will notice that all male scientists refuse to accept the fact that this was the beginning of life as we know it. Yes, the female was responsible for setting up civilization. The male just found another single-celled organism, pretended that he was king of the pool of water, bought gaudy furniture and expected plenty of sex for doing nothing more than belch in eight different notes.

The female, on the other hand, began organizing other cells. Experiments were done with less dominant cells for many years trying to come up with something more than what they already had. Soon, their experimentation proved to be a success. The single cell was no more. Women could produce multiple-celled organisms for the first time.

The males were furious. How could this lowly female organism, which had been kicked out of the pool just millennia ago, have multiple organisms? Try as they might, it just wasn't possible for the males to duplicate the feat. It's not as if they didn't try every chance they got to achieve multiple organisms but they never could. Oh, they'd claim that they didn't have any problems and could produce a multiple organism whenever they wanted, but they could never prove it.

But life was more than just multiple organisms. It required structure, touch and affection. Breeding grounds were set up to achieve optimum results. Thus, life began to evolve into more complex beings. In time, they took on different sizes and shapes. They developed limbs and soon began to crawl and walk. But tragedy struck and life was forever changed.

A huge meteor struck the earth. All would have been fine except that the best breeding males were at ground zero and all were killed. This left but one male on the planet. He was badly misshapen. He had three legs; two large ones and this small thing in the middle. Also, his breasts were flat. Tragically, the perfect look mastered by the females had come to a sudden end. The females decided that instead of waiting thousands more years to develop another perfect looking male, they would have to make do with the only one left. Breeding has its risks and those risks were taken.

Soon after breeding as much as he was capable, the one and only male was found dead one day. He was crushed to death under what we would say looked to be a replica of a 1957 Chevy. That left no living males on the planet, only one hundred pregnant females. The first offspring, as feared, had the same deformities as the deceased male. The females, deciding that all life has a purpose and exercising their more delicate nature, let the new freaks live. Faced with a decision to terminate life or continue breeding, the decision to continue was made. So the flawless look the females had mastered and multiplied with unstoppable success had forever ended.

Mass reproduction was now the norm. The population swelled, more changes occurred and soon the modern Homo sapiens as we know them were everywhere.

- 3 -
VENUS AND MARS:
AN IMPLAUSIBLE BEGINNING

The popular fiction about women coming from Venus and men coming from Mars is quite laughable when you think about it. My scenario, In The Beginning… (Chapter two), makes a lot more sense when the differences between the two sexes are closely compared. Still, just for argument's sake, let's assume I am wrong and see what life would have been like on both Venus and Mars.

A day in the life of:

VENUS

Venus is the second planet from the sun and source of the largest estrogen deposits in the entire universe. The planet is named after the goddess of love and beauty and is populated solely by women. Medical research on Venus has established beyond a doubt that estrogen is the source of splendor and contributes immensely to forming good-natured and well-adjusted individuals. Estrogen is also linked to greater life spans and the average life expectancy on Venus is eighty-six years. Everyday life on Venus is considered to be laid-back; lounging around while eating fruits and vegetables, enjoying conversations and intellectual wisdom. Venusians place emphasis on nurturing and supporting life. Education is a high priority but with the help of all their estrogen, degrees from colleges are unnecessary as their thought processes and cranial absorption levels are far superior to any other life form in the galaxy.

Venus has its share of interplanetary travel. The Venusians quickly invented space travel and continually learn from other beings around the universe on how to advance their own technology. A great variety of aliens regularly visit Venus. Their own worlds had been in conflict for years and they felt that estrogen therapy would end their suffering from war, famine and disease. The Venusians never demand money for their estrogen; it's naturally abundant and money is nothing but an object to fuel competition. Rather, they prefer to trade knowledge with every alien race they encounter and have what many species consider the perfect society. The only debate they ever engage in is whether or not to change the name of their planet to Utopia.

MARS

Mars is the fourth planet from the sun and source of the largest testosterone deposits in the entire universe. The planet is named after the god of war and is populated only with men. Not the little green men with pointy things that fiction conveys. At least not the green part. Unfortunately for men, their medical research links testosterone to aggression and violence, not to mention premature baldness and an average life expectancy of only fifty-five years. Speaking of premature, their studies also link an overabundance of this male secretion to premature ejaculation. But they are unconcerned with something as petty as coming too soon. They have land to fight over, ideology to protect and weekly competitions to prove who is the best.

Many aliens who visited Venus wrongly believed Mars to be a mirror image, except that men are on the planet and not women. Martians are too busy fighting each other or trying to win races to formulate ideas to better their lives. The first aliens who landed were not greeted with open arms and flowers as they had been on Venus, but rather were arrested on vagrancy charges and had their ships and technologies confiscated.

What happened when they found each other:

The Martians eventually found the Venusians by traveling to Venus in a stolen ship outrigged with sub-woofers and Dolby surround sound. The two worlds clashed on virtually everything; they had nothing in common. The Venusian scientists tried to extend their greetings by promising to research testosterone and its effects on premature ejaculation and aging. The Martians eagerly awaited their findings but set a one-week deadline for the answer. That didn't give the Venusians enough time to find a cure though, so the problems persist today.

The Martians desperately wanted to invade Venus and conquer its inhabitants but their invasion was ill timed. Every weekend the Martians wanted to invade just happened to have some sort of championship game scheduled and everyone knows that beings with testosterone must see every sport to its conclusion, especially when a championship is on the line. The final invasion plans were permanently shelved when the Indy 500 conflicted with the attack blueprint.

See what I mean? Could Martians and Venusians ever get together long enough to agree on something as complex as lifetime relationships? Not a chance. In The Beginning… (Chapter two), is the only plausible explanation for men and women being where they are today.

- 4 -
THE CAVEMAN COMETH

Men have significantly evolved since prehistoric times when they used to live in caves. Caves were their homes and a place where men first learned how to draw on walls. Recently, though, the meaning of "cave" has shifted from a place to live, to a subconscious plane of rational thought. A cave is not, as John Gray suggests, a psychological manifestation of a fragile ego that needs soothing or a physical destination to mull over a troubling episode in one's life. This idea is nonsense.

The roommate of a good friend of mine, who swears by the Men are from Mars philosophy, claims he needs to go into his "cave" whenever he's faced with something difficult that needs to be thought through. Now, really! Men need a place to sulk after losing an argument or placing an entire paycheck on the wrong horse. That's the way they were raised. They don't show their feelings because they interpret feelings as a sign of weakness. I can't believe that their behavior can be changed with a suggestion about visiting a cave.

Men do have caves but not the kind psychologists are referring to. Women have vast, expansive caves, which may be the ulterior motive men have by saying they want to spend more time in them. Most men have very little interest in visiting their own caves, even for a second. (Unless they're sent to prison and then it's cave roulette in the showers.) If a man brags that he enjoys going into his own cave, then he's incredibly gifted, if misdirected. One man I know said he'd been in his cave for the better part of four years. Now there's a man who needs a different hobby!

As long as this "cave" notion is going to be around, we should consider calling this new and improved creature a "caveman." Beware that the caveman has a particular way of expressing himself, often saying one thing and meaning something entirely different. It would be like any woman telling her husband that "I'm going to the store and I'll be right back." They both know that she'll be gone for hours and will return with eight bags destined for the top shelf of the closet. That's not what she said but her words were a phrasal mirage. The following are what a caveman will say to you and how it should be interpreted:

The Fabulous 50

Caveman says: "I'm OK. I'm perfectly fine."
Caveman means: "I've got twenty-four hours to come up with $500 or my bookie's gonna break my legs."

Caveman says: "I don't believe it!"
Caveman means: "My team won! My team won!"

Caveman says: "It's no big deal."
Caveman means: "My team lost! My team lost!"

Caveman says: "I don't consider it to be a problem."
Caveman means: "Just last year I could stay hard for two hours straight!"

Caveman says: "Are you sure?"
Caveman means: "You really trust me to go to the beach by myself?"

Caveman says: "You better ask your mother."
Caveman means: "I have no idea and am incapable of making a decision."

Caveman says: "My God, that was incredible!"
Caveman means: "That's the first time I've ever been in a Ferrari!"

Caveman says: "You're pregnant? That's great!"
Caveman means: "What are the non-extradition countries again?"

Caveman says: "I'm a little disappointed right now."
Caveman means: "Who the hell is Bob?"

Caveman says: "My wife doesn't understand me."
Caveman means: "She's still pissed off about my last affair."

Caveman says: "I was listening to you. It's just that I have things on my mind."
Caveman means: "I was wondering if that redhead over there is wearing a bra."

Caveman says: "I'm getting more exercise lately."
Caveman means: "The batteries in the remote are dead."

Caveman says: "You expect too much of me."
Caveman means: "You want me to stay awake."

Caveman says: "You know I hate to go shopping."
Caveman means: "You're going to make me hold your purse when you're in the dressing room."

Caveman says: "That's woman's work."
Caveman means: "It's dirty, difficult and thankless."

Caveman says: "It would take too long to explain."
Caveman means: "I have absolutely no idea how it works."

Caveman says: "We're going to be late."
Caveman means: "Now I have a great excuse to drive like a lunatic."

Caveman says: "Take a break, honey, you're working too hard."
Caveman means: "I can't hear the ball game over the vacuum cleaner."

Caveman says: "That's interesting, dear."
Caveman means: "Are you still talking?"

Caveman says: "Honey, we don't need material things to prove our love."

Caveman means: "I forgot our anniversary again."

Caveman says: "I was just thinking about you and got you these roses."
Caveman means: "The girl selling them on the corner was a babe."

Caveman says: "What did I do this time?"
Caveman means: "What did you catch me doing?"

Caveman says: "I left plenty of gas in the car."
Caveman means: "You might actually get it to start."

Caveman says: "You know how bad my memory is."
Caveman means: "I remember the lyrics to all the Rolling Stones' songs, the phone number of the first girl I ever kissed, the license plates of every car I've ever owned, but I forgot your birthday."

Caveman says: "Football is a man's game."
Caveman means: "Women are too smart to play it."

Caveman says: "I do help around the house."
Caveman means: "I once put a dirty plate in the dishwasher."

Caveman says: "I'm going to stop off on the way home for a quick one with the guys."
Caveman means: "I'm going to drink myself into a state of blindness with my knuckle dragging, chest pounding, pre-evolutionary buddies."

Caveman says: "She's one of those rabid feminists."
Caveman means: "She wouldn't make me coffee."

Caveman says: "I can't find it."

Caveman means: "It didn't fall into my outstretched hands, so I'm completely helpless."

Caveman says: "I just cut myself, it's no big deal."
Caveman means: "I hit an artery and will bleed to death before I'll admit I'm hurt."

Caveman says: "What do you mean you need new clothes?"
Caveman means: "You just bought a new wardrobe three years ago."

Caveman says: "Can I help you with dinner?"
Caveman means: "Why isn't it already on the table?"

Caveman says: "I'm going fishing."

Caveman means: "I'm going to drink myself stupid, stand on a bank with a pole in the water and pose no danger whatsoever to the fish passing by."

Caveman says: "Uh huh," "Yes, dear," and "Sure honey."
Caveman means: Absolutely nothing. It's a conditioned response like Pavlov's dog drooling.

Caveman says: "Let's take your car."
Caveman means: "My car is full of beer cans, girlie magazines, candy wrappers and is out of gas."

Caveman says: "We share the housework."
Caveman means: "I make the messes, she cleans them up."

Caveman says: "Have you lost weight?"
Caveman means: "I just spent our last $100 on a new three-wood."

Caveman says: "Woman driver."
Caveman means: "Someone who doesn't speed, swear, make obscene gestures, tailgate and has a better driving record than me."

Caveman says: "I broke up with her."
Caveman means: "She dumped me."

Caveman says: "I'm not lost. I know exactly where we are."
Caveman means: "No one will ever see us alive again."

Caveman says: "I brought you a present."
Caveman means: "It was free ice scraper night at the ball game."

Caveman says: "This relationship is getting too serious."
Caveman means: "I think I like you more than my truck."

Caveman says: "It's good beer."
Caveman means: "It was on sale."

Caveman says: "It's a guy thing."
Caveman means: "There's no rational thought pattern to it and you have no chance of making it logical."

Caveman says: "I heard you."

Caveman means: "I haven't a clue what you just said and I'm praying to God that I can fake it well enough that you don't spend the next two days yelling at me."

Caveman says: "You look terrific."
Caveman means: "I'm starving. Please don't try on any more outfits."

Caveman says: "I don't need any help."
Caveman means: "I am perfectly capable of screwing this up on my own."

Caveman says: "I missed you."
Caveman means: "I can't find my underwear drawer, the kids are hungry and we're out of toilet paper."

Caveman says: "You know I could never love anyone else."
Caveman means: "At my age, my weight and my income, no one else would have me."

Caveman says: "Of course I like it, hon, you look beautiful."
Caveman means: "Oh my God, what have you done to yourself?"

- 5 -
MYTH AND FACT

In *Men are from Mars, Women are from Venus*, Dr. Gray refers to men as having a Mr. Fix-It attitude toward communication and women as having a home-improvement committee attitude toward it. He states that men resent and resist being offered advice because they are the leader of the family and it's up to the leader to make the decisions. (I think that was General Custer's last sentiment.) Women have plenty of suggestions about everything under the sun, hence their "committee" label.

John Gray uses the standard psychological method of creating a certain scenario and scripting it around the point he is trying to make. Unfortunately, Dr. Gray's hypothetical situations lack credibility because they are too petty to be taken seriously, or they lack a point to the story, or they are unrealistic for the world in which we live. Properly scripted, some hypothetical situations are more real than others. My imaginary couple, Bill and Sue, will dispense errant scenarios and hypotheses (myth) with real-life conversations and situations (fact). By the way, if you don't like the names "Bill and Sue" that I've chosen, you may replace them with "B and S."

Myth: Men will have more respect for women if women keep their thoughts and comments to themselves instead of ruining the concentration men are struggling to preserve.

Fact: Bill and Sue were going to a birthday party. Bill was driving. It soon became obvious to Sue that Bill was lost as he continued to circle the same streets. But Sue once read that she shouldn't "offer advice" to her partner because it would be the same as insulting him. If she remained silent and left him to his own devices, he would have a greater appreciation for her. Unfortunately for Bill and Sue, this advice led to their untimely demise. Bill became even more disoriented and turned down the wrong street (Sue knew this but kept quiet) and they got caught in the crossfire of a gangland war. Their bullet-riddled car was found the following day. Sue apparently lived for a little while after being shot and had managed to partially burn her self-help book with a cigarette lighter before succumbing.

Myth: When a woman is talking about the rough day she had, the man should listen and offer heartfelt advice instead of just blowing off her concerns.

Fact: While that's wonderful advice for a perfect world, everyone knows what men are thinking about when their wives start talking about the day they've had:

Sue gets home from a grueling day at the office. Bill consoles her, knowing exactly what she needs:

Sue: "I've had such a hard day at work. It's so busy there."
Bill: "Gee hon, that's too bad. Maybe you'd like to have sex to get your mind off work?"
Sue: "No, I'd rather just put my feet up and relax for the evening."
Bill: "Tell you what. Let's have sex and think of new positions."
Sue: "I don't want to have sex. I want to relax."
Bill: "Sex is relaxing. Plus, you're the one on the bottom."
Sue: "Oh darn! I was so overwhelmed that I forgot to go to the store on the way home."
Bill: "What! You forgot my beer? Now you owe me sex!"

Myth: Setting limits and respecting each other's mutual boundaries is the key to understanding and respect.

Fact: Being able to compromise with each other's needs by respecting the inherent differences between the sexes is a bunch of gobbledygook. Here again we're faced with a clinical perspective while actually living in the real world. The only way a man will ever recognize the needs of a woman is for the woman to provoke the man into thinking with both heads at the same time.

Sue: "I want to take a vacation."
Bill: "I'm too busy to go. Too much work."

Sue: "That's okay. I'll go alone. I'd feel more comfortable on the nude beaches if you weren't there anyway."

Bill: "Uh, let me think this over for a moment." (He adjusts and scratches himself.) "I'd feel better if we, uh, I mean I, went with you. Is tomorrow a good day to leave?"

or

Sue: "I'm not feeling too well today."

Bill: "What's the matter? Are you sick?"

Sue: "I'm tired and a little cranky. I feel bloated."

Bill: "That time of the month, eh?"

Sue: "That's not a fair statement. You're generalizing a false stereotype."

Bill: "What else could it be? Women have a special time every month when they regress and turn into different people."

Sue: "And what about you?"

Bill: "I'm always on even footing. Men don't experience mind-altering changes or get periods."

Sue: "What about the time you tried to keep up with the kids for a month, playing street games and riding motorcycles all day? I think you even got a bad case of acne! Sounds to me like that was the male-only phenomenon called mid-life crisis."

Bill: "Actually, you are looking a little pale. Why don't you lie down for a while while I finish the chores? Forget I mentioned anything."

Myth: If a husband and wife go grocery shopping together, the wife should take direction from the husband, because he is head of the household and knows what's best for his family.

Fact: If you really think the family can survive on Pop-Tarts, Coors Light and motorcycle magazines let your husband shop for the family. Otherwise, give your husband the keys to the car so he can listen to the radio and stay out of your way as you plan a healthy diet for everyone for the rest of the week. Allow him to unload the groceries into the car, though, so both of you can tell the kids you shopped together.

Myth: A man's greatest fear is that he's either not good enough for his wife or that he's incompetent.

Fact: Talk to any man to dispel this myth. Men are already incompetent. You want proof? Try working for any male middle manager. And a man's biggest fear of all is having an evening with you all to himself, with you looking, feeling and performing your best while he's standing there unable to get his Little Buddy into the game. That's by far a man's biggest fear!

- 6 -
HE SAYS... SHE SAYS...

A successful relationship is built on the blocks of communication. This is true not only in personal relationships but in corporate relationships as well. A company that discourages communication among its employees is destined for failure. Likewise, an individual who either cannot or will not communicate with his or her significant other will more often than not experience frustration and anger instead of love and understanding.

When a man gets home from a tough day at the office and doesn't want to talk about it, Dr. Gray suggests that his wife should give him time to be alone and stay out of his way until he's ready to talk. She should go back into the kitchen where she belongs and stay there until he commands dinner and wants to talk about his day. This dysfunctional advice will eventually lead to a total breakdown in communication and understanding. Conversations will become convoluted; interaction and discussion will cease to have any real meaning.

In Mars and Venus in the Bedroom, Dr. Gray says that when a breakdown in communication occurs, a woman will begin to question the fundamentals of her marriage and her internal questions may become these rationalizations. Although I completely agree with that overall premise, I have problems with his scenarios. The italicized portions are Dr. Gray's scenarios while the rationalizations are more in line with a modern woman's reasoning:

She worries that: *There's a problem in their marriage and he doesn't want to be with her.*
She reasons: There's an inflatable woman under his side of the bed.

She worries that: *He must be angry with her.*
She reasons: He used his tractor to plow under her flower garden.

She worries that: *He's acting selfish and cares only about himself.*
She reasons: He just bought a third car and the other two still need work.

She worries that: *He's dissatisfied with her.*
She reasons: All their wedding pictures have her face cut out and Pamela Anderson's in their place.

She worries that: *He's lazy.*
She reasons: There's no other excuse for a day's worth of chili in his beard.

She worries that: *He's lost interest in her sexually.*
She reasons: Subscriptions to Playboy, Penthouse, and Hustler appear on the same credit card statement.

She worries that: *He has a deep underlying fear of affection brought on by his dysfunctional past and he needs therapy.*
She reasons: Anymore premature ejaculations and he should get the equivalent of sexual call waiting.

She worries that: *He's hiding something from her.*
She reasons: Someone's giggling in the closet and he won't let her look.

She worries that: *She got involved with the wrong man.*
She reasons: There's a prison jumpsuit in the attic.

Sometimes the man will open up a little, but his answers will be brief and distant. There are very few ways his answers can be interpreted, because a man who says very little with a lot on his mind, is a man who has some deep secret he's afraid you'll discover.

1. **She says: "How was your day?"**
    He says: "Fine."

    She *means*: "I can see you've had a rough day and I'm interested in hearing what happened."
    He *means*: "I got fired for spending too much time on the phone with my bookie."

2. **She says: "How did it go today?"**
    He says: "It was okay."

    She *means*: "I know you had a slide show today. How did it go?"
    He *means*: "Somehow our slides of that X-rated movie we made together ten years ago got into my slide projector."

3.   **She says: "Did they like your presentation?"**
     He says: "Yes."

She *means*: "Your black eye tells me something happened today."
He *means*: "I'm telling you, I just glanced at her breasts. She had no right to punch me and make me lose that account."

4.   **She says: "What's wrong?"**
     He says: "Nothing's wrong."

She *means*: "Where are your clothes?"

He *means*: "There's no point in telling you – you'd never believe me."

Men are known to regress when they desire something and know they're probably not going to get it. Sometimes men will want a new workbench when they already have one that works fine. But they saw a really cool one on television and now they must replace the one they've got. In a prime example of 'he says, she says', once a woman discovers the true nature of a man's material desire, she can allow him his indulgence and get something she wants in return.

Man: "I'm going to the store. I want to pick something up."

Woman: "Good. Can you pick up a gallon of milk? We're almost out. And another jar of peanut butter. I used the last this morning."

Man: "Actually, I was going to an electronics store."

Woman: "Why would you need to go there?"

Man: "I just saw some video games advertised on television and I want them."

Woman: "Wait a minute! Those are expensive! We should discuss a purchase like that."

Man: "I work hard and I want them. End of discussion."

Woman: "There are a lot of things I want that I don't get because we can't afford them. Anyway, since you bought that seventy-piece wrench and nut set, I hardly see you anymore on the weekends."

Man: "Well, what would you like to do while I'm playing my video games?"

Woman: "I'd like to go on a nude cruise with some of my friends. Get away from everything and relax."

Man: "You can have your cruise if I can get an extra action game."

Woman: "Great. I'll tell you when I'm leaving."

Man: "Did you say nude cruise?"

Woman: "Go buy your games."

Often, communication breakdown in relationships is just simple misunderstanding. There are many couples that have great communication skills and wonderful, lasting relationships, which simply misinterpret the signals the other party is emitting. Dr. Gray, in his infinite wisdom, loves to use imaginary conversations to prove his point. Although I prefer to rely more on empirical evidence than contrived commentary, I can't help but have my imaginary couple, Bill and Sue, reiterate the conversation they had the other evening.

This particular conversation involves the male being stuck with the female point of view (and therefore subservient), while the female embodies the male point of view (and therefore aggressive).

Bill just arrived home from work to find his housewife in a dither. Bill does not know how to properly communicate with his wife because all the self-help books he's ever read place the communication burden on the female. Sue, exasperated from her day taking care of the entire house, yard, kids and animals, is so befuddled she can't make Bill understand her point because he is incapable of appreciating her as an individual.

Bill: "What's wrong, honey? You seem tired."
Sue: "Nothing's wrong. I just have too much to do, as always."
Bill: "Oh."
Sue: "I just never seem to have enough time."
Bill: "Why don't you tell me about it?"
Sue: "All right. I still have laundry to get done, your shirts need ironed, I haven't fixed the lawn mower so I can't cut the grass, the car needs washed, and dinner isn't even started."
Bill: "What did you say? Something about dinner?"
Sue: "And I still have to take Billy to soccer practice and little Susie to ballet lessons…"
Bill: "Hmm."
Sue: "Were you listening to me?"

Bill: "Of course, honey. Billy needs to go to his ballet lessons. When's dinner?"

Sue: "You're not listening to me."

Bill: "I was listening. I just have a lot of things on my mind."

Sue: "So do you think you can help me with the kids? Can you handle dinner yourself tonight?"

Bill: "Hmm."

Sue: "Were you listening to me?"

Bill: "Yes, I was listening. What time did you say dinner would be served?"

Instead of Bill coming home and expecting his wife to fully understand all his needs, Bill needs to act less like a third world dictator who desperately needs time alone in his cave, and more like a responsible husband. Marriage is a two-way street; one-way thinking leads to a dead end. If Bill really knew his wife and understood the commitment of marriage, their conversation would have been short and to the point, and would have gone like this:

Bill: "What's wrong honey? You seem tired."
Sue: "Nothing's wrong. I just have too much to do, as always."
Bill: "Look, I've had a long, tough day and you've had a long, tough day. Let's prioritize the remaining tasks."
Sue: "That's a good idea. Right now, let's just focus on the kids and dinner."
Bill: "That's good thinking. I love you and we'll work together to get everything done."

Sue, my imaginary person, is a "contemporary woman," according to Dr. Gray. He contends that a woman's basic instinct is to mother and nurture her family; if she leaves them to advance herself as a human being by working outside the home, she becomes unstable. This "contemporary woman" develops a conflict within herself and asserts herself to her husband as if she were an equal partner. If Sue had remained at home, with no desire to work outside the home, she would have much better communication with her husband because she would understand him better. ***If you've ever searched for the definition of fundamentalism, this is it.***

The reason "contemporary women" are dissatisfied, is due to a lack of respect in relationships. I find it ironic that Dr. Gray has pinpointed communication as the number one reason for female dissatisfaction when he preaches techniques that de-emphasize communication in relationships. When a man and a woman accept each other as equals and work together toward the benefit of the entire family, communication is an unavoidable conclusion. Love, respect, understanding, desire and personal awareness lead to better communication, not the acceptance of a flawed philosophy.

- 7 -
THE LANGUAGE OF LOVE

Part A

Men offer us all many complexities. Sometimes they say things that are interpreted as offensive to women yet sound totally benign to other men. Then there are times when they want to say something that sounds completely benign but have an ulterior motive and are attempting to mask their activities or thoughts simply by saying anything. Women should be on the lookout for the man who says something without putting much thought into what he's just said. Here are a few common one-line responses women should give men when they know their man is up to no good:

Men say: "How 'bout we stay home tonight."
Women say: "Can I at least get something to eat first?"

Men say: "I'm gonna go work on the car."
Women say: "Is she pretty?"

Men say: "I need to stay late at the office tonight."
Women say: "Just use some protection."

Men say: "Is it hot or is it just me?"
Women say: "She wasn't wearing a bra, was she?"

Men say: "Is baseball a great game or what?"
Women say: "Did all that crotch-grabbing make you want to masturbate?"

Men say: "I'll see you in hell!"
Women say: "But we're already married!"

Men say: "Sometimes I don't know what's worse: My job or my wife."
Women say: "Compare them this way: In five years, your job will still suck."

Men say: "What does a cucumber have that I don't have?"
Women say: "About six inches."

Men say: "So what if I am underendowed?"
Women say: "You're the same as the Republican Party: I've lost interest in both."

Men say: "I get the feeling you haven't been listening to me lately."
Women say: "I'm sorry, did you say something?"

Men say: "Did you notice I laid new carpet?"
Women say: "Easier than learning how to vacuum, huh?"

Men say: "Do you feel like moving to another state?"
Women say: "I still get 50% you know."

Part B

Here are a few philosophical phrases men often spout when they want to impress their dates, girlfriends or wives. Women should consider the source before acting like they're impressed:

Show me the man who says, "Two heads are better than one," and I'll show you a man who doesn't think with the big one.

Show me the man who says, "It's the little things that count," and I'll show you a wife who wishes otherwise.

Show me the man who says, "It's not whether you win or you lose, it's how you play the game," and I'll show you a man who needs to work on his pick-up lines.

Show me the man who says, "God is smiling on me today," and I'll show you a man who just took his mother-in-law to the airport.

Show me the man who says, "I'm green with envy," and I'll show you a man looking at a Rolex while wearing a Timex.

Show me the man who says, "A picture's worth a thousand words," and I'll show you a man looking at a Playboy centerfold.

Show me the man who says, "Baseball is better than sex," and I'll show you a virgin.

Show me the man who says, "I never met a man I didn't like," and I'll show you a man whose girlfriend has never been hit on.

Show me the man who says, "I came, I saw, I conquered," and I'll show you the winner of a bragging contest among drunks.

Show me the man who says, "Haste makes waste," and I'll show you a man who's an expert at foreplay.

Part C

Men choose a particular vocabulary when they place personal ads. Although we would like to believe that men speak from the heart and practice truth in advertising, experience proves otherwise. Try answering one of their personal ads and you'll find that their adjectives are not based on reality. Listed in alphabetical order are common catch phrases men often use in personals to describe themselves with the actual meaning next to it in parentheses.

40-ish   (53-year-old in search of 24-year-old)
Adventurer   (Has had more partners than you ever will)
Affectionate   (Needy and looking for a mother-figure)
Artist   (Fragile ego badly in need of massage)
Athletic   (Sits in La-Z-Boy and watches ESPN)

Average looking   (Strange hair growth in nose, ears, and on back)

Communication Important   (As long as it's sports-related)

Distinguished-looking   (Wears a hairpiece and smokes a pipe)

Educated   (Will treat you like an imbecile)

Employed   (On management track at McDonalds)

Enjoys The Arts and Opera   (Snob)

Financially Secure   (I will spend money on you when I feel like it, and in return I will expect you to obey my every whim for the duration of your mortal life)

Free Spirit   (Will sleep with your sister)

Friendship First   (As long as friendship involves nudity)

Fun   (Quick with the remote and a six pack)

Good Looking   (Arrogant dickhead)

Honest   (Pathological liar)

Huggable   (Overweight, more body hair than Grizzly Adams)

Intelligent   (Can locate Canada on a map)

In Search Of Slim, Attractive Female   (Need someone eye-catching to offset my insecurities)

Light Drinker   (A six-pack a night and a case on weekends)

Likes Romantic Walks on Beach   (I'll say whatever you want to hear to get laid)

Mature   (Gray and balding)

Open-minded   (Wants to sleep with your sister, but she's not interested)

Physically Fit   (I spend a lot of time in front of mirrors admiring myself)

Poet   (Once wrote a poem on a bathroom wall while constipated)

Professional   (Owns a tie that mom picked out)

Reliable   (Never misses a playoff game)

Romantic   (Looks better by candlelight)

Self-employed   (Jobless and I reek of chili)

Spiritual   (Once went to church on Easter)

Stable   (Boring)

Thoughtful   (Will say "please" when demanding a Heineken)

Virile   (Can read three Penthouse forums without passing out)

Wants Soul Mate   (One step away from stalking)

Young at Heart   (Would like to be seen with a teenager)

- 8 -
COMPETITION AND SPORTS

Men dominated sports for ages. Ever since there was enough interest to cheer them on, men have been playing them. In Roman times, they would fight lions and compete with each other in games similar to what we now call the Olympics. Then, men often performed in the nude, which I'm a proponent of reinstating immediately.

Men cope with stress by playing sports and competing with each other. They prefer to forget their real problems and instead focus on lesser problems, like who's favored to win the NASCAR race and not worry about how to pay this month's mortgage. In order for a man's sport to flush his system of stress and aggression, the man must be able to enjoy his sport without any distractions from anything or anywhere else.

Dr. Gray's contention that men compete with each other and, when the game is over, revert to their calm, tranquil selves and will reconnect with their partner is absurd. When was the last time a man was able to watch a game on television and not relive the game hours after it ended? The fiery, ten-car pileup; the game-winning home run; the last-second field goal; the free throw with one-second left on the clock. No matter when the game officially ended, your husband will relive the moment for hours.

Men like the game of baseball so much because it reminds them of sex. (You might say both are American pastimes.) In baseball, as in sex, there's first base (kissing, endlessly fumbling with her bra), second base (hands on her breasts, removing her panties), third base (deep penetration), and finally, home run! (Orgasm—he scores!). When an umpire shouts "batter up!' it's the same as subconsciously telling a man to get an erection: batter up! B-o-i-i-i-n-g! Even the "count" (balls and strikes) remind men of their own equipment. A decisive count for the pitcher and favorable count for the batter is two balls and one strike. My, doesn't that sound familiar! Also, baseball and masturbation go hand in hand (pun intended). When men get together to "play ball," batters often compare bat size, as a means of deciding who has the best grip on his own equipment needs. If you're not very good at playing ball or you carry a small bat, you have a propensity to "strike out." Baseball games often take three hours to play and although men have difficulty lasting more than ten minutes in bed, it seems like three hours to them.

Most women I know also enjoy some of the professional sports men like to watch. Professional football is a good example. Granted, it's a bone-crushing sport and the average career is a scant three years, but check out those uniforms. Lots of bulges and pads. Hmm. Seems like there are more bulges than pads...I think I'll keep watching! Although I'm not a fan of rugby, I once watched in amazement as these men played football in very tight, very skimpy shorts. But rugby never caught on in this country because men see the same things we do on television. How many men do you know who want to be caught drinking beer and watching a rugby match alone?

There is a sport men can watch and not feel like they're part of the competition. That's because the same men who get together to shoot baskets and throw around a football, would never even consider trying to emulate professional wrestlers. I hesitate to use the word "professional" and only do so to identify the "sport." True competitions and sports are not choreographed and scripted. If you catch your husband watching professional wrestling, chances are he'll feign displeasure with what's on television. He may even try to futilely locate the remote, indicating he needs it to change the channel. But when you leave the room, the channel is never changed.

Unfortunately, there's another "sport" that men like to do. Hunting and fishing are masquerades for the sole purpose of killing. I don't know one person who claims he hunts or fishes for relaxation and then acts like he's relaxed afterwards. Hunting and fishing involve the taking of life. When a person takes a life, he feels even more inadequate than he did before he pulled the trigger or yanked the fishing line. To believe that four men going on a hunting trip to kill wild animals will return more relaxed and better adjusted is a fallacy. Although Dr. Gray juxtaposes modern day hunting and fishing to our ancestors of ten thousand years earlier, including his contention that men who hunt and fish will feel more relaxed, the situations are hardly related.

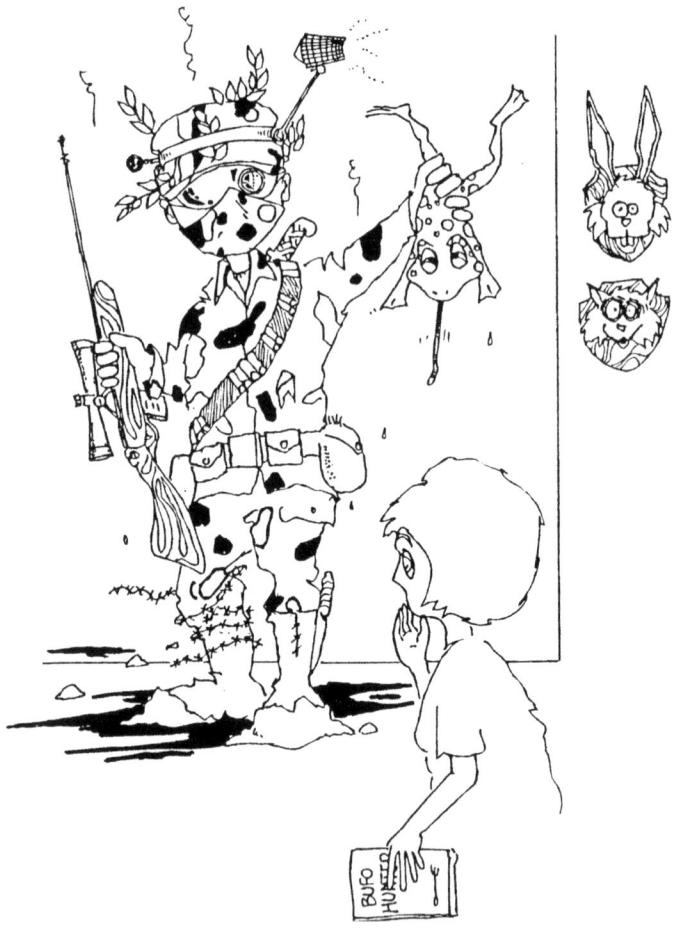

Humans used to have to hunt and fish for their very survival. There were no supermarkets or corner grocery stores, and no factory farming. Humans can no longer use that 'hunters and gatherers' excuse (with some rare exceptions). Men often say they hunt for only the biggest and strongest animals in the herd, so the rest of the lesser animals can mature and dominate. Unfortunately, natural selection doesn't work that way. If you kill the strongest animal in a herd, the herd becomes weaker because its leadership has been temporarily lost. Lost leadership has been known to decimate an entire herd.

If every man who now spends a long weekend killing game would spend that time with his wife and children, imagine the world we would have! Children would have more time with their fathers, wives would earn more respect for their husband's prowess around the house and husbands would appreciate how much work the stay-at-home mom really has to do. Appreciation leads to understanding, which leads to respect, which leads to a better marriage.

- 9 -
MODERN COMMUNICATION SKILLS

According to Dr. Gray, the primary responsibility for good communication is placed on the woman. It's up to her to remember the four P's to ensure the best communication in a relationship. The last time I checked, a relationship required more than one person to achieve success. (I don't know how John Gray can be thought of as helping people improve their lines of communication when he advocates that the responsibility lies with the woman while the man gets to play dumb.)

The four P's he speaks of are: pausing, preparing, postponing, and persisting. Both parties are supposed to recognize and understand the four P's for modern communication to work, but only the woman needs to remember them. Conversely, men need only to remember the four D's: ducking, dodging, disarming and delivering. He also states a relationship works optimally when both parties are doing their best to achieve results. If the four P's are water then the four D's are oil, and I don't see the two of them getting together and sharing each other anytime soon!

Here are the four P's for today's modern woman:

1. Pause

A. Without a doubt, the most important button on the DVD remote control.

B. When he asks whether or not you had an orgasm, pause for effect and say he should try again because you're not sure.

2. Prepare

A. Have all the food and preparation instructions on the counter before you leave for an evening with your girlfriends, or your husband and kids will starve.

B. If you think your husband is seeing another woman, start siphoning a few bucks out of the bank account…just in case.

C. If your husband comes home with a dozen roses, prepare to spend all night on your back.

3. Postpone

A. The engagement ring is wonderful, but you need another month to decide.

B. If he's attempting to enter his cave, quickly postpone what you were going to tell him and suggest therapy.

4. Persist

A. If he refuses to put the seat down, put a fuzzy cover on the lid that makes the seat fall down.

B. Toilet water is not supposed to be yellow – tell him to flush every time.

C. Tell him that his body odor is not turning you on and that civilized people use deodorant.

Here are the four D's for today's modern caveman:

1. Ducking

A. All the time, baby! (Sorry, I thought number one started with an F.)

B. Flex those abs, keep them in shape, so you can duck when she throws something at you and not strain a muscle.

2. Dodging

A. Keep those legs muscles in good condition, for that's the only way to dodge well.

B. Figuratively, every time she asks you to take out the garbage, tell her how young she looks – anything to dodge the subject and delay the inevitable.

3. Disarming

A. Calm, soothing words, maybe she'll remember to put the safety on or lower the gun altogether.

B. Kleenex is made from trees and a sensitive man does his best to ensure the survival of trees; ergo, men are not supposed to use Kleenex.

4. Delivering

A. You deliver your payload; nine months later she delivers a baby. Fair tradeoff.

B. You become a pizza delivery driver, thereby fulfilling a boyhood fantasy (dad would be so proud!).

- 10 -
CONVERSING WITH A MAN

There's a right time and a wrong time to talk to a man. If there's nothing going on in a man's life, stay away from him. Don't bring up any subject on which he might want further discussion. To do so would be a disservice to yourself. The best time to talk to a man is when he's fully engrossed in something that is near and dear to the hearts and minds of all men. Sports are far and away the best examples but you need to know which subjects to discuss during which sports:

The World Series (preferably the 7th game). This is the best time to discuss a new wardrobe. Men are quite content with the one pair each of underwear, socks and T-shirts they own so they can't comprehend the need for anyone else to own anything more. Discussions usually turn into arguments and the wardrobe is shelved unless the man's attention is diverted. Nothing better than a 7th game to divert attention. Bottom of the ninth, two on, two out, home team down by one…and you're about to get anything you want!

The NBA Playoffs. A great time to talk about jewelry, as it's more expensive and controversial than clothing. Men do not understand the elegance of wearing earrings and necklaces in addition to a nice watch. Watching the NBA will help your cause as professional basketball players wear as much jewelry as humanly possible when they are not playing. Your man's subliminal conscious therefore recognizes the need for jewelry, but his mind and subliminal conscious don't talk to each other. Also, don't worry about having to repeat yourself when he interrupts what you're saying after a spectacular dunk – he's not listening to you to begin with. Just calmly tell him you'll be gone for a few hours and then leave.

The Super Bowl. (First half only.) Hair has importance, too. It's been four months since your last perm and now is the best time to get another one. Just be sure to tell him sometime in the first half. By the second half, when one team is blowing out the other and he's just waiting for the funny commercials the beer industry creates to promote their products, you will already have his "permission" and are well on your way to the hairstylist.

NHL Finals. Home improvement. Watching ten men with sticks chase each other and a puck around a frozen pond is exciting to men. Casually mention that it's the right time of year for him to clean the yard and to help you plant a garden. He'll just nod and say things like "whatever" and go back to slobbering in front of the television. No, he won't remember promising to do any home improvement but he'll assume you're telling the truth because he knows you talked to him during the game and he answered but he can't remember what he said.

While he's engrossed in sports, it's also a good time to play mind games on him. Make a snack for him and say things like, "Strychnine's ready! Come and get it!" He'll make his way to the table, sit down and start eating, never taking his eyes off the game. About two bites into his snack he'll ask you if you said "strychnine." Just smile. It's more fun that way.

As soon as the sports are over and the day winds down, he'll want to indulge his Little Buddy, and cons you into having sex that night. Take advantage of the situation! Play hard-to-get and "give in" just as he's becoming exasperated. Halfway into his routine, you can ask him about the car:

Sue: "Hon, I'd like to talk about getting a new car. You know, trading in what we have now for something newer."
Bill: "Yeah, sure. Buy whatever you want. Let's try this position…"

Using subliminal conversations to get what you want

If talking to your husband during sports gets you what you're looking for, you don't have to wait for a sporting event. You can use your intellect in another way on any day of the year.

Bill: "Hi. How was your day at work?"

Sue: "Fine. I new purse was busy but I'm not very tired."

Bill: "Good to hear. What time is dinner?"

Sue: "I haven't really new dress thought about it. Maybe new watch around seven."

Bill: "That's a good time. Are the kids coming right home after school or going to a friend's house? I can never remember."

Sue: "Little Susie is coming right new shoes home but little Billy is going to play manicure baseball with some friends."

Bill: "Well, just as long as he makes it home in time for dinner."

Sue: "I was going to hop in the perfume car about 6:45 and pick him up to make sure he gets spending money home on time. Is that you cook all right with you?"

Bill: "Yeah, that'll be great." (Pausing) "Actually, why don't you let me pick him up? Here, take some money and go shopping for yourself for a change. You could use new shoes, a new purse, maybe some jewelry. The thought just sort of popped into my head. And don't worry about dinner. I'll cook it."

- 11 -
DUCKING, DODGING, MOANING, GRUNTING

Men need help ducking and dodging difficult subject matters. Dr. Gray's readers are left with the impression that women are put on this earth to serve men, so women are required to help men duck and dodge. Men feel the need to do this when they are preoccupied with their own lives and can't listen to what anyone else has to say. A man will send out signals by saying things like, "I need some time alone," and "I'll be right back," or, God forbid, "I'm going to my cave."

If a man decides he must spend some time in his cave, women are required not to say anything negative to him, lest he may want to stay in there longer. Women should avoid saying things like, "Why do you do this when we should be talking?" or "We don't spend enough time together," or "You don't love me," or even "This is the third time this week you've been to your cave!" Of course, any couple foolish enough to believe this masterful manipulation is destined for trouble because both parties have accepted that men are incapable of communicating. Don't let your man duck and dodge your questions. Part of life is overcoming mistakes and faults—ducking and dodging responsibility sets a poor example for our children. True marital salvation has nothing to do with one party slinking off because he either cannot or will not communicate with the other.

Marital communication has regressed in the last few years, thanks to men believing they need to take cave time to duck and dodge a problem they don't wish to confront. It's very important for a woman to be able to ascertain when a man cannot converse because he's either about to enter or hasn't yet exited his cave. Dr. Gray cautions women about approaching men with difficult questions; a woman must know her man's signs before she asks him something. Bill and Sue, my imaginary couple, show you how difficult it is for a woman to follow this advice:

Sue: "Last night, right after dinner, I asked you what plans you had for our anniversary next weekend. You abruptly said you needed cave time and disappeared. Are you still in your cave?"

Bill: "I don't know. What do you want to talk about?"

Sue: "I wanted to know if you prefer chicken or fish tonight."

Bill: "Oh, okay. I'm out of my cave now and I prefer fish."

Sue: "Fine. Say, yesterday in the car, Billy blurted out that he wanted to know what masturbation was. Can you talk to him about it?"

Bill: "Sorry, I can't. I just went back into my cave."

Sue: "But I thought you said you were out of your cave."

Bill: "I was out until you asked me that tough question on masturbation. Then I had to duck back into my cave again."

Sue: "All right." (Pause) "I suppose I can't ask you about your plans for the football playoffs, either."

Bill: "Sure I can answer that—I'm out of my cave again."

Sue: "What is this hang-up with you and your cave? Can't you face a difficult question anymore?"

Bill: "Sorry, I went into my cave for that question. But I do plan on getting together with the guys this weekend and watching the playoffs."

Sue: "I see. I suppose that if I ask you about that vasectomy you promised you'd get last month, you'll have to visit your cave again."

Bill: "Now you're catching on!"

Sue: "Well here's a really difficult question for you: Tonight, between 8:15 and 8:45, I'll have just enough time between chores for a wild sexual encounter. Now can you accommodate me or do you have to visit your cave again?"
Bill: "Cave? What cave?"

While there are many different ways for men to duck and dodge a question or sensitive topic, women should be more attentive to the little sounds men make when women are trying to have a conversation. A man will moan, grunt and interject nonsensical language as a means to allow a woman to think she's being heard, when in fact he's trying to ignore her. While John Gray may call them "reassuring sounds," more often than not women know exactly what men are trying to say:

He moans: "Hmm."
He means: "I'm thinking really hard for an answer you'll believe."

He moans: "Oh."
He means: "I have no idea what you just said or how to reply."

He moans: "Uh huh."
He means: "I was listening to you—sometimes I snore when people are talking to me."

He moans: "Oh, hmm."
He means: "Do you really think the back seat is too small?"

He moans: "Hunnh."
He means: "I thought I could wash my workbench and get it clean with one of your sponges."

He moans: "Ouch!"
He means: "Did I hear you say that dress cost $200?"

He moans: "Huh."

He means: "I have complete confidence that you'll take care of whatever you just said."

He moans: "Wow."

He means: "You mean I have to put soap in the washing machine to get clothes clean?"

He moans: "Whoa."

He means: "That reminded me of my prom night."

He moans: "Oooo." (as in moon)

He means: "You're right, I think I do have herpes."

- 12 -
GETTING IN TOUCH WITH YOUR "SIDE"

Dr. Gray advocates new relationship skills for men and women in his book, Mars and Venus Together Forever (*Relationship Skills for Lasting Love*). Relationship skills are crucial to a successful marriage and Dr. Gray's advice is that women and men must refocus and redirect their energies toward either their female or male side. While this is not a new concept, his spin on the subject is original. Of course, you have to accept his theories and conclusions on male/female relationships for his suppositions to apply.

Dr. Gray provides his reader with a list of twelve things both men and women (single or married) can do to nurture their male or female side. It's interesting to note the style of wording Dr. Gray has used for his suggestions. Notice he tells women what they can do (active wording – all his first words end in "ing") while he suggests what men can do (passive first wording). I have used his list of all twelve for both sexes (the italicized portion is his) and changed the examples provided after each suggestion to reflect a more modern society.

12 Ways Women Can Nurture Their Female Side

1. *Taking more time each day to share in non-goal-oriented ways about the problems of her day.* Have lunch at least once a week with your lover.
2. *Getting a massage or some kind of nurturing bodywork every week is extremely valuable.* Now he can't complain if you spend too much time and money at the beauty parlor.
3. *Talking on the phone and/or staying in touch with relatives or friends.* At five cents a minute, you can talk forever!
4. *Making regular time for prayer, meditation, yoga, exercise, writing in a journal, or working in the garden should be*

observed with great commitment. Spend your time praying that someone can write a self-help book that offers real, and not imagined or contrived, advice for relationships.

5. *Creating a work style that supports her feminine side.* Paint your workstation pink and scream sexual harassment if your boss says anything about it.

6. *Getting at least four hugs a day from friends and family members.* Go to the gym and make friends with all the buff bodybuilders and insist on lots of hugs.

7. *Taking the time to write thank-you notes for the support you receive from others.* Write to Simon Cowell and tell him you love his British accent.

8. *Varying routes home from work.* Spend three hours commuting on back roads instead of the normal two hours on the freeway, dramatically increasing your chances of an accident.

9. *Becoming a tourist in your own town and regularly taking a mini vacation.* Pretend the local fruit stand is really part of a nude beach.

10. *Joining a support group or visiting a therapist to make sure you can share your feelings freely without being concerned*

about your professional reputation. You'll need a therapist after reading *Men are from Mars, Women are from Venus*.

11. *Setting aside one evening a week for yourself.* If you can set aside one evening, why not set aside all seven?

12. *Listing everything that needs to be done and then putting in big letters at the top, "Things that don't have to be done immediately."* Things like cooking dinner, making sure the kids get off to school, waking your husband up in time to go to work – little things like that.

12 Ways Men Can Nurture Their Male Side

1. *Spend time with other men in competitions.* Peeing off the deck is a safe and highly satisfying competition.

2. *Go to action movies.* Experience the violence your male side craves! Just don't treat your wife as the Terminator target.

3. *Take cave time in your relationships.* End every discussion you can't handle or every difficult question by saying you need cave time.

4. *If you don't have a sexual partner and you want to be more in touch with your male side, then practice self-control and don't masturbate.* You'll soon be in touch with your true male side, all right. Just remember, global terrorists never masturbate.

5. *Make sure you exert your muscles every week.* Lift a beer, open a bag of chips, and masturbate with both hands.

6. *Make sure your life doesn't get too comfortable and cushy.* No one likes to see someone else live the American Dream and "have it all."

7. *Try each week to do random acts of kindness – for others you care about or complete strangers.* Steal a television and give it to your mother-in-law.

8. *When you are upset or angry, don't punish others; instead, focus on your breathing.* Be sure to stand on a soft rug so when you pass out from hyperventilating you don't hurt yourself.

9. *Make a list of all the things you most enjoy doing.* Don't feel bad if everything on the list has the word "sex" or "beer" in it.

10. *When something needs to be done that won't take a lot of time or energy, do it immediately.* Better yet, tell your wife to do it.

11. *When you feel afraid to do something that would really be good to do, feel the fear and do it anyway.* Lots of people have run with the bulls in Pamplona, Spain, and with prosthetics nowadays, you'll hardly miss your left arm.

12. *Practice containing your anger.* I'm sure going to all those action movies can teach you a lot about containing anger.

- 13 -
LOVE AND ROMANCE:
TWENTY SIGNS A MAN WANTS SEX

In Mars and Venus Together Forever, Dr. Gray informs women about the twenty most popular signs and signals men give off when they are looking for sex. Naturally, Dr. Gray believes a woman should learn to recognize these signs and indulge the man whenever he pleases, regardless of how the woman feels at the time. I'm providing many of the same tried and true examples, along with other signs in parentheses that show a man's desperation in getting sex.

1. He puts on your favorite song (no matter how much you know he hates it).
2. A candlelit dinner (and all the candles are from forgotten birthdays, some with old frosting).
3. He brings you flowers (they're the daisies you planted last weekend).
4. Tells you your hair really looks good (even though you're wearing a hat).
5. He washes the dishes by hand (and dries them with the seat of his pants).
6. Flushes the toilet (after using it just once).
7. Says, "I love you" (when you bend over to pick up something on the floor).
8. He writes to you (and misspells your name).
9. Coos you if you're upset (and leaves his tongue out for an extra long time).
10. He brings you chocolate (and all the filling has been sucked out).
11. Comments that your clothes look nice (and he's been in the room with you for more than an hour).

12. Plans something more than an hour in advance (and in writing).

13. He thought of you on the way home (after hearing an advertisement on the radio for angel cakes).

14. He's overly affectionate, with hugging (and he's not in bed…yet).

15. Spontaneous hugging (he finishes by squeezing your butt).

16. He looks into your eyes when you talk (and never once looks at your breasts).

17. Uses the remote's mute button (even on the beer commercials).

18. Lets you finish every sentence (even when you're talking during the sports scores).

19. He uses Kleenex or a paper towel (instead of his sleeve).

20. Calls you to tell you he'll be a little late getting home (so you'll know when to meet him at the door in a teddy).

- 14 -
AROUSAL

Mars and Venus in the Bedroom (A Guide to Lasting Romance and Passion), another in a long line of follow-ups by John Gray, focuses mainly on sex. I was shocked by the graphic content in this book! It covers how men and women like to have sex, when's the best time to have sex, how to tell when your partner's aroused, different kinds of sex, mood swings...the list goes on. Dr. Gray tells his readers how to tell when a man is aroused. He explains the chemistry and spontaneous changes a man will experience when he's aroused, as well as those same changes in a woman, and how to spot someone who's letting passion get the best of them.

While I admit staring and drooling are common traits men unconsciously display, there are other mannerisms as well. Personally, I think it's all too easy to tell when men are sexually aroused.

You take your average, love-starved man to a busy shopping mall. Make him hold your purse and stand just outside the store entrance while you go inside the store and watch where he can't see you. (The reason you make him hold your purse is so he has absolutely no chance of scoring with another woman.) Sexual arousal in a man placed in this type of situation is virtually guaranteed because many of the other shoppers are attractive young women. He'll pace around, taking in the sights, until he sees someone and becomes aroused.

His slow, plodding pacing suddenly becomes quick, with little baby steps and frequent tight-circled turns. This is his futile attempt to divert his attention from the stunning redhead coming out of Victoria's Secret. When she drops her bag, spilling the black-laced bras to the ground, it's the perfect opportunity for the man to stare. It's okay, he rationalizes, because all the other men in the mall holding purses are staring too. His breathing, once a slow, methodical inhale/exhale, becomes rapid and shallow. He will have to take refuge on a bench to keep from hyperventilating. His mouth will involuntarily open slightly and the tip of his tongue may protrude. Saliva collects at the corners of his mouth. His arousal is almost complete!

Now his hands turn ice cold and his palms sweat. If he stands up now he's going to have a big problem (especially if he's wearing sweats), but if he continues to sit, his problems double. Men who sit down all the time are viewed as wimpy and pussy-whipped by other men, so his only option is to stand up. Fortunately, he's holding a rather bulky purse. Feigning interest in a store display, he hurries to the front window with the purse held squarely in front of his groin. The man, in less than thirty seconds, is fully aroused!

You, still keeping an eye on him from inside and your purchase finished, feel this is the perfect time to exit the store, so you grab your man by the arm and start walking away. He'll have to surrender the purse (no choice there) but he'll immediately replace it with your bag of purchases from the store. Whew! Close call for the man!

Women, as Dr. Gray tells us, commonly think men want only one thing: sex. Unfortunately, Dr. Gray is a man and doesn't realize or can't admit that women are absolutely right with their thinking. Men only want sex. He brings you flowers? He wants sex. He buys you chocolate? He wants sex. He comes home with an edible bra and panties? Well, that's pretty obvious. Foreplay? A prelude to sex.

Being able to tell when a woman is aroused can sometimes be a mystery. This type of mystery ranks right up there with the Seven Wonders of the World. A candlelit dinner (lobster and steak), licking each others' fingers, expensive perfume, striptease to the bedroom, oil rubbed on the bodies, hot, sweaty, animalistic sex for an hour. This is something he'll never forget and something you may not even remember in a week. Why? Because what is sexually arousing to a man sometimes is not sexually arousing to a woman.

Women need a long, drawn out buildup of passion to become sexually aroused. All a man needs is a short skirt. But women *must have* a feeling of sense, respect, worth, commitment, love, dignity **and** passion to experience the same feelings men have when they see long, endless legs.

The key is not for women to accept men's sexual arousal faults, as Dr. Gray suggests we should do, but rather for men to mature beyond the caveman mentality and value sex for what it truly is: mutual appreciation for the other person, expressed in the most intimate form known to mankind. Sex is sacred and should be treated as such to derive the most pleasure.

10 Major Turnoffs That Women Should Avoid Saying

Dr. Gray provides a short list of turnoffs for women to memorize and avoid saying to their partners to dampen his sexually aroused state. As usual, there are no suggestions for men to consider what may turn off women. I've repeated his ten turnoffs that women should avoid – the italicized parts – and added in parentheses what a woman actually means:

1. *"You're not doing it right."* (Foreplay doesn't mean jumping on me.)
2. *"I don't like that."* (Balancing empty beer cans on my breasts is not cool.)
3. *"Ouch! That hurts!"* (Maybe hot wax on the nipples wasn't such a good idea!)
4. *"Don't touch me with that!"* (I told you that a bra made from cactus wouldn't arouse me!)
5. *"That tickles."* (Great. I can expect to be touched there every morning from now on.)
6. *"Not like that."* (When I said I wanted to try new positions, I wasn't referring to a spinning chair.)

7. *"Not yet."* (If I make you wait just a few minutes longer, you might be more appreciative or you may give up altogether.)
8. *"Not there."* (When I said I wanted you to French kiss, I meant with our mouths.)
9. *"I'm not ready."* (I just walked in the door from work.)
10. *"What are you doing?"* (Are you asleep already?)

Quick sex, or "quickies" are they are commonly referred to, are a natural part of life. Usually, when one partner wants to have sex and the other one doesn't, a compromise is reached in the form of a quickie. One partner's lust is satisfied for the moment and the other partner didn't have to take much time away from the task at hand to provide the other with what they desired. Sometimes, though, one partner wants to have sex and it just isn't the right time for the other. Enter John Gray. He suggests women should make quickies guilt-free, thereby automatically supporting a man in feeling free to initiate sex, even when the mood is not right for her.

This is not to say that women never want to have sex. Women enjoy good sex just as much as men do. Dr. Gray has been kind enough to provide women with responses they should use when their husbands ask for sex and women are not in the mood. In other words, he's providing yet another list of submissive suggestions on how women should continually give in to a man's wishes.

Let's turn his advice around. Let's use this same logic and see how a man would react to Dr. Gray's suggestions of passivity and observe what answers a man can give instead of simply saying no. These examples purposely aren't very humorous because they're being used to refute an absurd point.

She suggests: "I am really turned on. Let's have sex."
He suggests: "Actually I'm not in the mood, but let me caress your breasts."

She suggests: "I've missed you. Let's make some time to have sex."

He suggests: "I've had a brutal day – let's have a quickie after the game."

She suggests: "I have some time for sex. Do you want me?"
He suggests: "I could schedule you for a quickie now and maybe a full session tomorrow."

She suggests: "You want to go upstairs and spend some time together? Maybe we could snuggle?"
He suggests: "I just don't feel like it. But I'll set up the DVD with a hot movie if you like."

She suggests: "Let's have sex tonight."
He suggests: "I've got a pounding headache. How about I just eat you out?"

She suggests: Nothing out loud, but reaches over and begins fondling him.
He suggests: "Don't worry about me tonight. Break out that power tool and make the lights flicker."

Only someone who believes that marriage is an unequal partnership would expect a man to react like this when he doesn't feel like having sex. But Dr. Gray concludes that's how a woman should react to a man's suggestion of sex, even when she isn't in the mood. If this is what he truly believes, then marriage is not equal to him. I have read several of his books and not once have I found an example of a man "giving in" to a woman's desires. A successful marriage is built on a give and take relationship, not a one-size-fits-all approach.

- 15 -
OLD LOVE LETTERS

Dr. Gray believes that a way to invigorate a listless relationship is to write love letters back and forth. For the most part, love letters reinforce our feelings for our partners and are a simple way of expressing the caring we have for each other. It may be puppy love (as in the case of teenagers and young adults) or true love (as in the case of a husband or wife of many years telling the other through simplistic means how they still feel). I disagree with Dr. Gray's point that a physical relationship that has grown apart can become closer with a simple love letter. Maybe it's worked for him, but how well could it have worked? He has been divorced, after all.

I just happened to be rummaging through my cedar chest in the attic one day when I found some old love letters and letters of advice from men and a few from women. I wonder how Dr. Gray would interpret the feelings of these people?

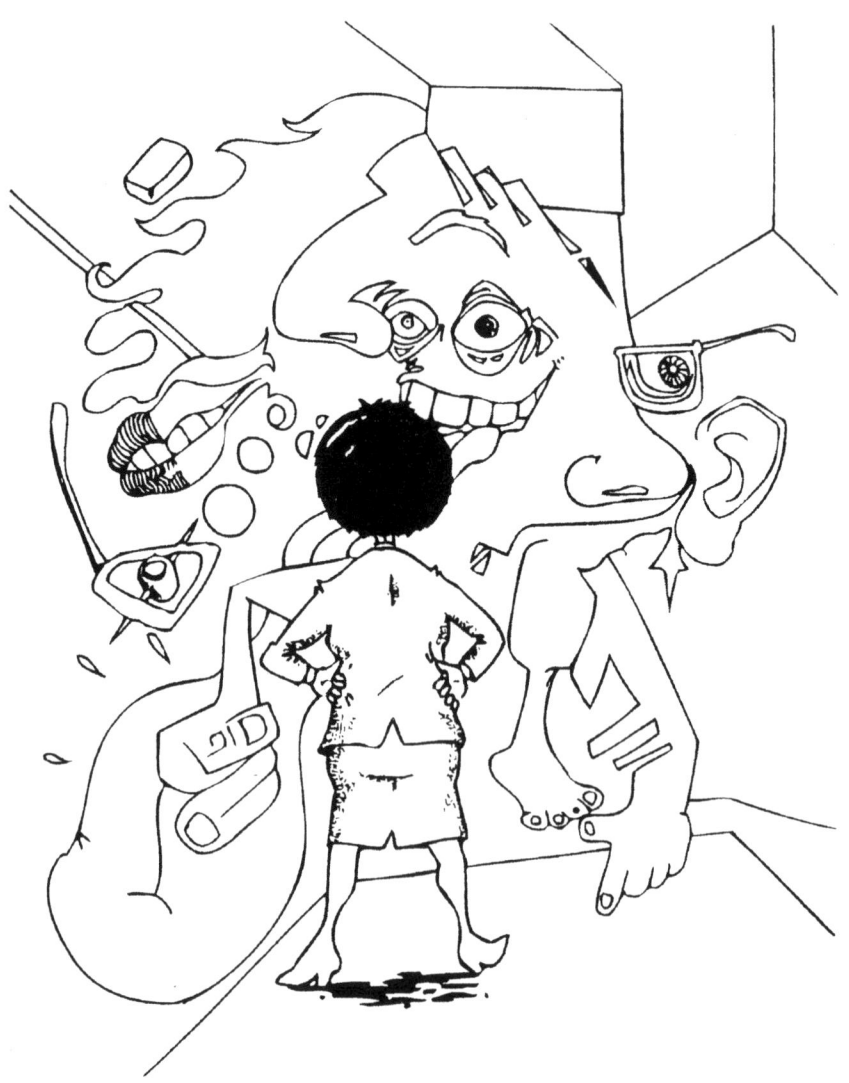

December 25, 1972

Dear Katherine my love,

I guess I owe you an apology. I thought the portrait you commissioned me to paint came out great! Maybe you see yourself in a different light but I think two noses are attractive on a woman, especially when one of those noses is in the middle of the forehead. The crooked, drooping eyes, the square mouth with orange teeth, the yellow tongue and blue hair made your triangular face a sight to remember. That's how I'll always see you. If you want your money back, I'll give it to you. But this thing's going to be worth something someday.

Love,

Pablo Picasso

May 2, 1981

Katherine,

I really liked last evening. I thought you were charming and beutiful. The dinner was grate, wasn't it? I know yer a little upset over all the ettention called to us but I can't help it. Yes, I should have been paying more ettention in the lobby so the steward didn't have to call my name four times before I heard it. I was jest so caught up in yer beuty. I jest didn't get a chance to xpress myself because of all the snikering around us. Even in skool I could never consentrate long enuf to learn how to spell rite. Maybe u can put that past us.

Luv,

Ben Dover

April 17, 1987

Ms. Black,

I appreciate you writing to me for advice on your relationship problems. That is what I'm here for, no? There's nothing like a short German woman with an annoying accent to turn men on, no? The first thing you must do to attract men is to think like a penis. Men love their penises and the more you think and act like a penis, the more men will want to get to know you. You should even try to find a man named Dick – why else would a man name himself after his member if he weren't truly in love with his penis, no? How do you go about doing this?

You must first try to imagine yourself having a penis. When I wake up everyday I think to myself, "What kind of penis do I want today?" If your answer is the same as mine, which is usually a ten-inch schlong hanging between my legs, then you're on the right track. Now try to imagine your brain in the tip of the penis and think with it all the time. That's what men do, no? Now you're thinking like a man and men will like you more.
Hope this advice helps.

Good luck,

Dr. Ruth Westheimer

November 31, 1990

Katherine:

I want to extend my thanks to you for traveling all the way to The White House just so we could talk about the biography I considered having you write. But after witnessing what you said at Friday night's dinner, I'm afraid that I must find someone else to write about my life.

I want to correct you on a number of mistakes you made. First, Canada is south of us and Mexico is north. The Pacific Ocean isn't really an ocean – it's that big lake in Utah. The Gettysburg Address is the address of the Lincoln Monument. Hemp was a quarterback and played football in the NFL. And finally, it really is spelled p-o-t-a-t-o-e. (My aides want me to tell you that everything written here is taken out of context.) Now if you'll excuse me, I have to get back to helping run the country.

Regards from second in command and a serious presidential candidate,

Dan Quayle

P.S. Since you told me how much you like the beaches, as soon as I get elected President, I'm going to ask Hawaii if they're interested in statehood. Hawaii can be our 52nd state!

March 10, 1996

Katherine,

I know how much you must miss me but my affairs keep me busy. There's some controversy in Arkansas that Tyson Foods, one of the state's largest employers and a huge contributor to my campaigns, has been polluting a river with runoff from their farms. I'll go down there, meet with a few of the ladies who started the story, and make the whole thing blow over.

I've got a fundraiser I have to attend this evening with some chinamen. Know any good capitalist pig jokes? Ha-ha, just kidding. Tomorrow morning, an old friend of mine, Paula, is stopping by with her attorneys to identify something that belongs to me. After that, I'll be welcoming a new intern to the White House. My aides tell me this intern has a big mouth – I'll have to put that to good use.

Looks like I'm in trouble with my secretary now. She was reading a column from the Washington Post out loud to me last week and somebody wrote something about "assumed supposition" and I thought she said, "assume the position." They sound alike, don't they? I don't know, I think she's just a blowhard and I should know, right?

I've been going through some of my old love letters and I sure do know a lot of women! But you know you're my one and only.

Presidentially yours,

William Jefferson Clinton

March 30, 1997

Dear Katherine,

Last month, when you told me this White House job would suck in a few months, you were right. It sucks every day – sometimes several times a day. And there are other hardships, too. I have to wear really nice clothes all the time and if anything happens to one of my dresses I don't even have the money to clean it. My nice blue dress has this awful mayonnaise stain on it. At least I think it's mayonnaise.

Also, the pay is pretty bad. The other day I was trying to make some extra money helping to park cars out back, thinking maybe I could score a few extra tips, but all I got was the shaft. It seems like every world leader thinks they can stiff me. I've got a few ideas about how I can make money but I don't want my squeaky-clean reputation ruined like my dresses.

Yours truly,

Monica Lewinsky

June 15, 1999

To stupid Katherine,

I certainly didn't do this but someone intercepted the letter you sent to *Dear Abby* and sent it to me instead. You are such a stupid person for writing to her for advice! I can only assume you have been listening to me for years and you should know by now that whatever problems you have are caused by you, you alone and no one else. You're such a stupid person if you don't already know that!

That's not to say I'm singling you out as stupid. All women (except me) are stupid. If it weren't for men to tell us and show us (except me) everything we're supposed to do with our lives, women would never amount to anything (except me).

Here's what you should do in your troubled relationship: The man is in charge. He always has been in charge. Don't listen to your instincts – you don't have any that make any sense. No women do (except me). Fall down at the foot of your man, kiss his feet and then give him a BJ if he wants one. Then cook him dinner. If he doesn't like it, it's *your* fault. You have to accept responsibility for *your* actions (unless you posed nude when you were young and the photos are published on the Internet – that could happen to anybody and certainly wasn't *my* fault!!!).

Feel free to give me a call sometime when I'm doing my show and I'll chastise you on national radio. That's how I treat all women (except me) because all women are stupid (except me). Then you can thank me on air like all the other stupid women do who call my show asking me for advice in their relationships.

Piously yours,

Dr. Laura Schlessinger

- 16 -
COMMON TOPICS OF DISCUSSION

In *Men are from Mars, Women are from Venus*, Dr. Gray hammers across the point that women should be submissive when asking for support and being told they aren't going to get any. He even states that after a man has said no, women should "graciously and simply say 'OK'." If you ask your husband to do something either for you or around the house and he refuses, perhaps because he read a self-help book that encourages that sort of response, give him something to think about using responses like these:

The scenario: The baby's diaper needs changed and you ask him to do the job.
He says: "I'm busy reading the paper. You do it."
You say: "OK, fine. He's wearing an 18-25 pound diaper – let's see if it'll hold that much."

The scenario: The dog needs to go to the vet to get his rabies shot.
He says: "I don't feel like doing it."
You say: "OK, fine. If he bites you and you die from rabies, just remember that I get everything."

The scenario: Little Susie needs help tying her shoes before she goes out to play.
He says: "This is the 9th inning and the score is tied. I can't help her now."
You say: "OK, fine. She'll probably trip over her shoelaces and knock out her two front teeth. Then she'll never get married and will live at home until she's thirty."

The scenario: He's working on new shelving, you're cooking dinner and the kids need picked up.

He says: "These measurements are crucial. I can't drop everything just for the kids."

You say: "OK, fine. There's a bus line where they are. If they miss the bus let's hope they're not kidnapped walking home."

The scenario: Mrs. Jones, one of the kids' teachers, wants a parent-teacher conference.

He says: "I'm not interested in going."

You say: "OK, fine. I have four loads of laundry to do. Let's send your brother Frank, the recently paroled rapist, to meet Mrs. Jones."

The scenario: Tonight's a great night to go to a movie.

He says: "I'll do what I want with my evenings, you do what you want with your evenings."

You say: "OK, fine. I'm going to see a romantic movie and I'm taking your boss with me."

The scenario: You both get home from busy days and now he's watching television.

He says: "I've had a busy day at the office. I'm too tired to help with dinner."

You say: "OK, fine. Would you like the garbage cooked al dente or well done?"

The scenario: After dinner, there's a pile of dirty dishes to be loaded into the dishwasher.

He says: "Dishes are the definition of woman's work. You do it."

You say: "OK, fine. I apologize in advance for breaking every dish we own."

The scenario: It's been quite a while since the two of you sat down and talked.

He says: "If something was worth saying, you would have said it by now."

You say: "OK, fine. I'm still not sure who the father is anyway."

The scenario: You just got home from shopping and want him to bring in the groceries.

He says: "The new rule is, whoever does the shopping also brings them in and unpacks."

You say: "OK, fine. As long as it's new rule making time, you have to shower before we have sex."

The scenario: The trash needs taken out.

He says: "I'm head of the household and I'll decide when it's time to take out the trash."

You say: "OK, fine. I'm sure the chicken wrappers will wait for you."

The scenario: Saturday rolls around. You want to go dancing and he wants to see a movie.
He says: "I'm the man of the house and I say we're going to a movie together."
You say: "OK, fine. But I'm picking the movie and we're going to watch something that has either Bette Midler or Barbra Streisand in it."

The scenario: It's been a long week and you want to spend some time cuddling together.
He says: "Cuddling is something men do before they're married, not after."
You say: "OK, fine. Just remember that women can go months without sex."

The scenario: The car was in the shop and is now ready to be picked up and has a hefty bill.
He says: "I'm not taking you there. It's your job to see it's fixed, picked up on time and paid for."
You say: "OK, fine. I'll walk there and turn a few tricks on the way."

The scenario: It's the evening before you're both going on vacation and you want to talk about the trip.
He says: "There's no reason to talk. Don't you have ironing to do?"
You say: "OK, fine. I'm leaving for the Bahamas in the morning – I'll make sure your connections are screwed up. Have fun in Anchorage."

- 17 -
THE FOUR SEASONS OF LOVE

John Gray concludes *Men are from Mars, Women are from Venus* with his four seasons of love. Basically, he juxtaposes men's and women's desires and how they should feel with the season in which they should feel them. It struck a sour note with me after reading his book about how women should play the part of servant to their husbands and then about how men and women can enjoy true love and wonderful relationships if they time everything to the right season. I felt this was a weak attempt on Dr. Gray's part to oversimplify relationships and to sugarcoat his philosophies.

Therefore, I submit these Four Seasons of Love for your consideration.

Springtime:

After a winter of hibernation, he's ready to get it on with anything. Hope springs eternal; it's like falling in love all over again. But the twice a day's can wear on a girl. Therefore, you must be able to convincingly fall asleep in the early evening to avoid petering out (pun intended). He'll never wear out, or so you think. You're partially right. He can go several times a day for months (as you'll see) but every engine can't last forever, especially if he never checks the fluids.

Summer:

Early summer is when he plows your field, and you're more than happy to plant a garden. The trouble is that he wants to plow every day, sometimes even several times a day. You can't have a happy garden that way. Summer is also the sticky time of year. If he wants to plow and you won't let him, be sure to carefully inspect your ladies magazines. If they have a much-read look and the underwear advertisements are a bit tattered, you may have a problem on your hands. If the pages stick together and are faintly stained, you *definitely* have a problem. It's not the humidity. Summer is also the time when it's hot and sweaty. After spending a day over a hot stove or stuck in an office without air conditioning, there's less energy to expend getting it on. Plus, after seeing what he's capable of doing in the springtime and now with your magazines, it's just as well.

Autumn:

His engine's gone 60,000 miles without a rest or an oil change. If he abuses his engine it's going to conk out on him if he's not careful. (Years ago, he was told he'd go blind if he abused his engine, but that wasn't enough of a scare.) This is your opportunity to begin resting. Don't go full-blown hibernation yet – save that for winter. This is when he begins winding down and you both can enjoy passion at its finest. The weather is cooler and it isn't sticky anymore. If your new magazines still have that "summer problem" then it's not your only problem. Perhaps an early frost is all he needs to settle down into a regular routine.

Winter:

Now men know where the term "winter of discontent" comes from. His engine has been resting and he's revving it up. He wants to take the stick shift for a test drive every night. You, though, have an ulterior motive. This is wintertime, a time for hibernation, when you need to save your strength for more important things. Sex can therefore be used as a bartering tool. He'll even reveal his true nature after an extended holdout on your part. This is your opportunity to open his eyes to the fact that there's more to life than sex. Expect his emotions to gyrate; if you're successful, though, his gyrations will be worth it. Patience and tolerance are considered virtues. Just make sure he doesn't try to visit his cave during this mini-hibernation. If that happens, you can forget about instilling him with virtues.

- 18 -
QUEENS AND KINGS

Is it possible to prove that a queen has more importance in our world than a king? I believe it can be proven with just a few examples. Unequivocally proven.

Take England for example. For hundreds of years they have had queens and kings. When one or the other dies, there's great fanfare as to who will take the crown. But it's just been the last hundred years or so that the spotlight has been so closely focused on the royals. In the past, only nobles were invited to the ceremonies to see the new crowning. But in this day of media coverage and instantaneous accounts from around the globe, a marriage, a death or crowning is big news.

Who's the King of England right now? I would look it up but I don't feel like doing it. I know who the Queen of England is. It's Queen Elizabeth II. Everyone knows that. And my point is well on its way to being established. The Queen of England seems to have far greater importance than the king. Sure, the Prince of Wales is Charles but who really cares about that polo-playing, skirt-chasing, globetrotting, big eared and even bigger egotistical son of which king? Is Charles the one who's spied on with a hidden camera in a weight room? Do photographers follow him around from beach to beach trying to get a shot of his bare chest? Of course not. They'd do that for a queen or a princess, but not for a king or a lowly prince.

Chess is a game for nobles and even us commoners. The pieces to the game are: eight pawns (most of us can relate to this piece), two bishops, two rooks, two knights, a queen and a king. Without question, the most powerful piece on the board is the queen. She can make virtually any move that any of the other pieces make and is the most feared of all. Sure, only the king can be checkmated, but doesn't that sound just like a king? Maybe if he could move more than one space at a time he wouldn't require so much support from the other pieces, especially the queen. And should the other side take the queen, well, the game is practically over. The king is naked without his powerful protection and soon collapses without the support he needs to survive.

For centuries now, mankind has given items of great importance or significance the name of "she." When volcanoes erupt, we say, "There she blows!" Climb the same mountain when it's calm and you're climbing "her." Even planet earth is given the "she" connotation and called "mother." Ask a mariner about the Titanic, the "unsinkable" luxury ocean liner slowly rusting away on the bottom of the Atlantic Ocean, and he'll say something to the effect of, "She's found her resting place now." Notice how he won't say, "He's resting." Maybe men feel more comfortable saying they got aboard a "she" than a "he." While many men may brag about getting on board the Queen Mary, few would brag the same way about mounting the King Fred. I can understand that logic. And it's not just mountains or boats. Every inanimate object that we place value on has the designation of being affiliated with women.

How about a bee colony? Social bees, the kind most of us are familiar with, are members of colonies in which they cooperate with others to build the nest and to feed and protect the young. It came as no surprise to me to learn that females have the greatest responsibilities in a bee colony. There are three distinct classes of bees and the sex of the bee in most species is determined by whether or not the egg is fertilized. Fertilized eggs develop into females. The sexually mature, fertile females are called queens; the sexually undeveloped females are called workers. The workers do all the work described above. So what do the males do?

Unfertilized eggs develop into males and male bees are called drones. They do not work and exist only for the possibility of mating with females. Now honestly, doesn't this sound just like a male? They do zilch, expecting the female to do all the work around the nest and raise the young at the same time, then, when the time is right, all they want to do is have sex. Queen bees dominate the nest and are the most powerful and respected female of all.

Everything presented in this chapter points to the fact that queens are preferred over kings in the grand scheme of things. Queens are coveted in nature, and only females can be queens. Case closed.

- 19 -
BELCHING, BURPING AND BREAKING WIND

How does your husband tell you that the meal you spent two hours cooking tasted great and was perfectly filling? He could say, "That was a great meal, honey, thanks a ton" or "I'm stuffed. Where did you ever learn to cook that well?" or better yet, "After a meal like that I'll do the dishes." No, that's too direct for men. What they say instead of all that is, "Brrraaaggghhh."

One humongous belch, loud enough for the neighbors to hear. Not only does his belch signify that he's full but that he's impressed with the meal. On the downside, that kind of a belch means that he's too stuffed to help with clearing or washing the dishes. All he has the energy for now is to make it to the couch and watch television for the rest of the evening.

The Man of the House is the Belch of the House. If you've got kids and they try to learn the fine art of belching at an early age, get ready for a war of egos. If you're sitting at the table, nearing the end of the meal and one of your kids bleats out the signal that he's finished, watch out. Your husband will stop eating and ask for an apology. You see, kids don't automatically comprehend the power implications of the mealtime ritual, so they have to be scolded. This only applies to male children, of course. Females aren't allowed to belch under any circumstances, and if they dare to try, it is understood that an apology is in order.

The belch from the man tells everyone else that he's done and that he is king of the household. Only the king is allowed to announce through implied means that he's about to depart the table. Your kids will eventually catch on, around the age of eleven, and maybe even take his place if he's out of town. Try as you might for an apology, it's futile. You don't scold your husband for his rudeness and the kids have noticed. No point in trying to enforce a double standard.

Burping, however, is something else. Everyone burps, even females, though ladies tend to be more discreet than males about this bodily function. A burp is short and to the point. If you had to put a burp into words, it would be a short definition out of the dictionary, whereas a belch is more like a topic in an encyclopedia. Men resort to their primordial roots when belching; it's their call of the wild. That's why females don't indulge in it. The louder and longer the belch, the more a man he must be (at least to other men). To women, he's simply a guy with way too much time on his hands.

Occasionally, the man may burp during a meal. More often than not, he'll excuse himself because it was unintended. He's saving up his gas, readying himself for the Power Belch. If he isn't finished with his meal yet, a premature Power Belch is outside the allowable rules. The only exception to this rule is if he's drinking beer with his meal. Drinking beer and burping go hand in hand, and the premature burps don't impair him from performing his window-rattling belch.

Naturally, once men have experienced the Power Belch they can't stop there. Though exercised less frequently, they can't resist an occasional Covert Belch, especially in mixed company during social gatherings with friends or long-time business associates. The Covert Belch is the act of expelling a large amount of gas through the mouth while trying to make as little noise as possible. His cheeks will puff out considerably and he'll release the gas like a slow leak from a propane tank. Don't get too close to this expulsion! Like propane, there's a price to pay for inhaling these emissions. Men who are pros at the Covert Belch can direct their poison to specific people, even across the table. You may be eating and get a whiff of something strong enough to bring tears to your eyes. Look up and if a man's eyeing you with a Cheshire Cat grin, you've found the guilty party.

Then there's the Firecracker Belch. The man will open his mouth wide in preparation for the explosion he's about to release. You'd expect the earth to shake when he finally releases it and you silently wonder why the contents of his stomach aren't all over the wall. The firecracker belch will usually draw the most applause from his buddies and even the kids.

Another common entertainment item is the Outboard Motor Belch. Outboard motors are famous for sputtering along and so will your man. He'll open his mouth about halfway and you'd swear that someone pulled an unseen ripcord from his back because this belch never seems to let up. He could choke to death during one of these and you wouldn't know it until he was finished and dropped dead.

Any belch or burp is always preferable to the next inescapable noise men love to make. Maybe it used to be a love call, but women grew out of it around the time we left the caves. Whatever the history that may be involved, farting is a man's passion.

I personally prefer the burp or a belch at the table to let me know he liked the meal. Men who break wind at the table have another agenda: They want to know the level of tolerance of everyone else they're eating with. If your husband rips one just ten minutes into dinner then he's either pissed off or he feels it's time to test the family. Anyone who waves his hand in front of his face or obviously holds his breath is a wuss. Do it too often and he'll cut you out of his last will and testament. This is serious stuff.

The bedroom is a common area for farting. But this is just so he can impress you. Men seem to feel it's necessary to fluff the bed sheets after letting an extraordinary one go. Trust me fellas, we were impressed enough by the sound! If the bed sheets really needed to be fluffed, then chances are that they'd need to be replaced, so don't bother. Impressing others should be saved for when everyone's engrossed in watching television.

The television is, by far, the most common arena for men to deliver their windy messages to each other. If I thought they were smart enough, I'd swear this was another form of language that they and they alone were able to comprehend. But they're not that smart. Believe me, if intelligence had anything to do with it, why would they try it with fire? Who would be so foolish to try to see a streak of fire shoot from their rear end? Men would, which is why they couldn't be communicating with each other.

Picture this: The whole family sitting around the television after enjoying dinner. Definitely an American setting. Something you'd expect Norman Rockwell to paint. I wonder how old Normy would paint your husband leaning to one side for a moment to "gaspress" himself? Don't expect an apology from him, ever. This is how men compete with each other. Women break wind too, I mean, everyone does, but we apologize for the interruption. Usually.

Men will get together to watch television or talk cars and about every five minutes one of them will fart. The louder and longer the better, as those get the most approval. The worst smell also gets honorable mention. I was once in a van with three other couples and we passed close to an open sewer (I presume). Before anyone realized the smell was from a sewer break, all the men in the van, including my husband, tried to take credit for creating the odor themselves.

Probably the worst place for your man to test the tolerance of others is in the car. Convertibles don't count unless it's winter and the top's up. Then all you convertible lovers are in the same boat as the rest of us. Forget about turning on the air conditioning or venting the car – it's too late. As you're vainly struggling to hold your breath, your hubby inevitably wants to converse. So he'll start a conversation as the kids are dying in the back seat. You, trying to remain stoic, ignore the green haze as it builds up in the car. If you roll down the window, then you're weak (in his eyes) and subject to even more fluffing that night. And should the kids roll down the windows then they have to put them up again, as he'll complain about how cold it is outside.

Those are the ones you hear. The Gas Chamber farts are different. You know it's your husband because nothing else smells that bad. Even though everyone in the car knows who did it, your husband will ask for the guilty party. As if bidding for gold at a dollar an ounce at an auction, everyone speaks up at once, denying that he or she is responsible. He'll get a kick out of this, but at the same time he's keeping a close eye on the kids. Should one not say anything, or worse yet, take credit for it, then your husband suddenly has a viable hunting partner.

Our kids will learn these bad habits and take them into adulthood where the cycle perpetuates itself. Although our young males may have to apologize for burping and breaking wind at inopportune times, you know it's not in their nature to do so. Little boys are famous for cupping their hands underneath their armpits and then flapping their arms up and down, trying to replicate that favorite male noise. The really good and daring ones will do it in class, where they'll get a note to take home to their parents. Have your husband sign it. He'll do so with pride. Maybe he'll even make a copy and hang it above his workbench in the garage. Like father, like son.

- 20 -
FORTY REMARKS THAT ONLY COME FROM MEN

1. "How do you know it's mine?"

2. "Yes, they itch all the time!"

3. "I'll do it after the game."

4. "I only read it for the articles."

5. "How can you be sure that's *my* hair in the drain?"

6. "This is really good, but you don't have to cook it again."

7. "Who says cholesterol's bad for you?"

8. "That'll put hair on your chest."

9. "I wasn't picking it!"

10. "I just don't understand why you need so much toilet paper."

11. "Smoking a pipe makes me distinguished."

12. "Well I think $200 for a putter is a great buy!"

13. "You don't need to flush *every* time."

14. "I'll handle it from now on."

15. "The first thing I notice about a woman is her eyes."

16. "Be patient. It gets bigger."

17. "You know I love my car...oh, and I love you, too."

18. "Beer *is* food."

19. "But I thought you *liked* getting a vacuum on your birthday!"

20. "The definition of perfect? Big enough for the hand and small enough for the mouth."

21. "Floss???"

22. "Obviously, this was imported latex."

23. "This is almost as good as *my* cooking!"

24. "I don't need a napkin. I've got my shirt."

25. "This'll just take a minute."

26. "It takes balls to do something like that."

27. "No, you can't buy me a new toothbrush. I'm still breaking this one in."

28. "You don't have to write it down. I can remember it."

29. "I wasn't sleeping; I was just resting my eyes."

30. "I love the way you eat a banana."

31. "It must be that time of the month."

32. "It's only dirty if it smells dirty."

33. "Damn, I'm good!"

34. "What do you mean gross? That's a year's worth of belly button lint there!"

35. "Mine don't stink."

36. "Imagine the time I'll save next December if the Christmas lights stay up all year."

37. "I'm happy with a girl, but when can you have a boy?"

38. "I fell in love with her personality."

39. "I can stay hard for hours!"

40. "Of course I remembered our anniversary! Let me go out to the car and get your present. Be back in an hour."

- 21 -
THE MILITARY

John Gray believes that men are inherently aggressive individuals, predisposed to want to fight and use combat as a means of settling differences. Although I haven't heard his views on women in the military, after reading his books I assume he's against them being there in any capacity.

To the military's credit, we have what we believe is one of the freest countries in the world because brave men, and women, have laid their lives down to defend freedom, liberty and justice for most of us. If it weren't for our armed forces, I would not be able to write this book, as freedom of expression would most likely be curtailed. That being said, and giving credit where credit is due, the military sets itself up to be ridiculed.

What has been the biggest military debate since the early 90s? Gays in the military. I find it hilarious when the generals and politicians start debating this issue. The press gets involved, congress is convened, the president is forced to take sides, people are upset and angry with each other over the very thought of individuals being gay and serving in the military.

Let me get this straight. Hundreds of young men all volunteer to start their military careers by eating, exercising, sleeping and showering with one another for six consecutive weeks. Well, if there were ever a scenario for someone to turn gay, this would be it!

Who in the world really cares if homosexuals want to serve their country by joining the military? Take two steps back and look at the issue from an unbiased standpoint. I think gays in the military would promote peace and may be the best thing for the world as a whole. Imagine entire armies made up of nothing but gay men and women. Do you really think they'd kill each other over petty ideology or some insignificant speck of land? I don't think so. A homosexual military would undoubtedly spend most of its time planting trees and flowers. The only fighting would be over whose begonias looked better or whether red rhododendrons should have been planted instead of white.

Even the uniforms would change. Drab green and olive fatigues would be replaced with puffy pink and white jumpsuits. That would make camouflaged jungle fighting impossible. Black combat boots would clash with the jumpsuits so they'd have to be replaced with yellow loafers. Survival suits might look more like morning bathrobes.

No, I seriously doubt a homosexual army would prove a danger. They might fight each other over eyeshade but I don't envision them killing each other over it. Serving your country and dying is not a joking matter and I'm not belittling those who have sacrificed their lives for our freedom.

Anytime a soldier dies in combat, it is a tragedy. With the world in such disarray, it's common for us to lose many fine men and women every year, even without a war. Many years ago we began honoring our dead with a twenty-one-gun salute, a tradition that still lives today. Why not a ten-gun, or a twenty-gun salute? Why is it twenty-one? If women ran the military (although I doubt a world run by women would require a military), I think we would have honored the dead with a twenty-gun salute. It's a nice round number and matches the number of digits: ten fingers and ten toes. Men give a twenty-one-gun salute because they have ten fingers, ten toes, and one penis. Long live the mighty penis.

Military terminology is so laughable that I can't help but provide a list of military terms and their real meanings:

About-face: The USA is 13 and 1 in wars. That's all the face we need.

All hands on deck!: Drop your cocks and grab your socks, it's time to exercise!

At ease: You can relax now and go back to picking your nose.

Grunt: The sound someone makes when they realize they've signed up for four full years.

AWOL: The first thing someone does after they grunt.

M.P.: The people assigned to bring back the people who have made grunting noises.

Basic training: A six-week course where men learn to intimidate through force and coercion.

Colonel of the urinal: Someone who exercises his right to freedom of expression.

Eyes front: What a female officer says to new recruits when they try to watch her as she's leaving.

Fire in the hole!: What happens to someone's penis, three days after having sex with a prostitute who has syphilis while on leave.

Flash suppresser: A condom.

Fort Bragg: A place where soldiers claim they're hung like bears and trained to act like them.

Forward ho!: Whores in the next village. Let's hurry.

K-P: The command given when the enlisted are allowed to relieve themselves.

Latrine duty: The Marines.

Sergeant at Arms: A sergeant with hands so quick that he can pinch a butt or put his hands up a dress and leave the room before anyone notices.

Ten - Hut!: A quarterback count intended to draw the defense offsides.

Training dummy: Anyone above the rank of sergeant.

Twenty-one-gun salute: What happens to twenty-one men when a *female* officer bends over.

Twenty-one-gun salute: What happens to twenty-one homosexuals when a *male* officer bends over.

- 22 -
BULLETS AND MISSILES

Ever wonder why bullets and missiles are shaped the way they are? Is it because they're more aerodynamically efficient being designed that way or was that the only shape men were able to think of? Bullets, missiles and other weapons of mass destruction are all in the shape of a penis. Go ahead – think it over. From early man, cave dwellers and on through the ages, it seems as though men can't get that shape off their minds.

But this thinking actually goes much deeper. Not only are their weapons the shape of their penises, but they'll go to war if someone else's penis is bigger than theirs! Isn't that why the Japanese attacked us? What reason did they have other than the fact that their stubs didn't even begin to compete with Mr. American Penis! So they sent their planes, with their bullets and torpedoes, and attacked us.

Big mistake! Not only did we have to respond to their aggression but our men had to answer to a small penis. Unacceptable! Of course, I don't have to retell history and recite how we dealt with them. But I will say that had women been in charge of the world's affairs, the Japanese never would have bombed Pearl Harbor. Oh, there would have been a fight all right, but it would have been more like a Friday night mud wrestling extravaganza: slapping, biting, yelling and screaming. But no killing.

For men, having bullets in guns and going out shooting is like taking their Little Buddy out for a night on the town. It's a chance for men to get together and do manly things, like shoot a gun. Maybe they'll even kill some small, defenseless animal, have it stuffed and put over the fireplace to show it off, telling some wild tale to their pathetic hunter friends.

Men have even established their own firing ranges. Men of all ages, and some women who like to experience the powerful sensation for themselves, flock to these shooting ranges around the country. They even have shooting exhibitions and contests to see who has the fastest and most accurate hand. As if they really needed contests to prove that! Don't be fooled. It's a fancy penis showoff. If bullets were shaped like vaginas do you really think men would act the way they do and shoot them off? Of course not! They'd sleep with them instead. No more war. Problem solved.

- 23 -
HOW TO PAINT A HOUSE
WHEN YOU HAVE A HUSBAND

Men don't like to admit it, but there are people who spend their entire lives painting things for other people. I know every man likes to fantasize that he, and he alone, is the only person in the world who can open a can of paint, use a paint brush and apply a colorful coat to whatever it is he wants to cover. Just have the Yellow Pages ready and marked ahead of time. He's going to need professional help if the house is going to come out right.

First, he waits for "the perfect weekend" to paint. Perfect has a lot to do with the weather, but usually means that either his sports team or any team isn't playing for a championship on television. If it's auto racing or a regular season baseball game then he'll listen to the radio while painting, only to rush inside to see the spectacular car crash or a home run on instant replay.

Second, if he has kids then the kids have to drop everything they have planned and help him paint. This usually means picking up the paintbrushes when he drops them or stirring the paint when it's open to keep the colors from separating. But he has an ulterior motive for using the kids. When he drips paint on the windows or knocks a can over himself, it's the fault of the kids. They weren't watching what they were doing or they were daydreaming or, the unthinkable, trying to find the phone book to call a professional painter.

Third, your husband must have everyone's cooperation to get the job done. This means that everyone is at his beck and call and everyone must assist him whenever he needs help. However, he is the only one permitted to take credit for actually getting something painted. Believe me, you had nothing to do with him getting the job done, assuming your hubby is one of the .001% that can actually paint something right.

Fourth, all his buddies have to be out of town and all the neighbors he talks to have to be away for the day. This is essential. Read on.

Men, for whatever reason, become color blind when picking out a shade for the house. When he convinces you that the whole house really does need to be blue, with a matching yellow garage, be forewarned that blue can turn into green awfully quick. And that yellow might get a little orange when it dries. But that's okay. You, after all, chose those awful colors and forced him to paint the house. That's after the paint has dried and he realizes his color mistake. If he actually got the right color or if it turns out to be a better shade than he'd planned, then it was his wisdom.

Men are allergic to ladders. They are also addicted to buying them, which makes for strange bedfellows. My ex had three ladders in the garage at any one time and had fallen off all three at some point. Every year he'd find a reason to get a new ladder and try like hell to avoid throwing one of his old ones away, even if the wood was split or the metal fractured from one of his many falls. Men are like birds that can't fly. Quite a dilemma.

This being the case, you need to expect your husband to fall off the ladder at some time when painting the house. If he doesn't fall, then something will fall from the ladder, like a full can of paint. Of course, it was the kids' fault, because they were the ones who stirred the paint and must have made it off balance. Also, if the ladder is wood and one of the steps breaks then again it was kids' fault because they must have carried it wrong.

If you've got a 2,000 sq. ft. house, your husband will predict that he'll be finished painting by noon, no matter what time he starts. Noon is lunchtime and all projects have to be done by then, no exceptions. I think there's a universal man's handbook somewhere that states this as rule number three, right behind numbers one and two, "I am a God" and "I pulled out early, it couldn't be mine."

You'll notice that your husband's brush strokes are better up and down rather than from side to side. It's due to all his hand exercises. Up and down, up and down. Side to side doesn't work. Don't bother asking him to explain this phenomenon – it's the same reason your son spends an hour in the bathroom and never flushes. All that practice inevitably leads to subliminal usefulness.

Men will always start the painting at the back of the house. The 99.999% know somewhere deep inside their bodies that it's going to be a disaster and it's better to hide their "mistake" from scrutiny so the professionals can cover it as they work.

Just two hours into the project, something will happen to make the man stop. There's something wrong with the paint or the kids aren't concentrating and he has to do their work for them. Whatever the excuse, there goes the $500 in equipment and supplies – he's calling a professional. No matter what the estimate, it's worth it because his "help," i.e., wife and kids, weren't up to the task.

He'll collapse on the couch in an exhaustive heap. Wow, what an effort! He's even too tired to go to the fridge for a beer and the cupboard for the potato chips. Sorry, dear, can't help with the dishes, gotta go lie down for a while. But that night he finds enough energy for an hour of mattress mambo.

In the end, professionals paint the house, and he brags to his buddies that he did it in less than a day with no help from the thankless family. The neighbors even make complimentary comments about how good his house looks and suggest that he consider painting as a part-time business. He'll take their comments literally and the next time something needs painted, there's no way he'll even consider hiring a professional. Hey, he painted the whole house before noon, what does he need a professional for?

- 24 -
ASKING FOR DIRECTIONS

As every woman knows, men are incapable of asking for directions. They insist on driving, knowing full well that they haven't got a clue where they are going. If you, the passenger, make the slightest bit of noise then it's your fault that he is lost, because you wouldn't let him concentrate on driving. No matter that the radio is blaring *Led Zeppelin*, it was your noise that drove him to distraction.

All he had to do when he became unfamiliar with the terrain was roll down his window and ask someone on the street for directions. But this would go against his nature and might alert other men that he had failings. Men must have secret postings where the names of those who admit fault are published for other men to see, thereby causing shame. Maybe those who admit fault have to buy everyone else a round of beer at the ballgame. That alone would cause men to keep their imperfections to themselves.

Take Lewis and Clark, for example. Their wives simply asked them to go down to the corner market and pick up a quart of milk for biscuits. Lewis was coming from the north, and Clark was coming from the south. They both missed the market by a block and when they met each other on the street, started talking about the local soapbox races and wandered west. Both men became so engrossed in the conversation that they walked for days before they realized they were lost.

Instead of admitting they had made a mistake, Lewis and Clark sent a message to President Thomas Jefferson and informed him that they were on an expedition and needed supplies. President Jefferson probably realized that they were lost but, being a man and covering for his fellow subordinates, authorized supplies and more men for this expedition. What is ironic about this so-called expedition is that an Indian woman named Sacagawea served as their guide. Sacagawea already knew the western area of the United States, as did the rest of her people. But because men, specifically white men, did not, then it had to be considered undiscovered. Maybe that makes sense just to men because it makes none to women.

Lewis and Clark finally made it to the Pacific Ocean, declared they had found the western part of the United States, and headed home. It took more than a year just to make it out west and about the same to get back home again. There on the doorstep of each of their homes, were their wives, still waiting for the milk their husbands had been sent out to get. Naturally, they had forgotten and had to be sent out again, this time with one of their daughters to make sure they could not only get the milk, but also find their way home.

Christopher Columbus is another fine example of a man getting lost because he wouldn't ask for directions. Columbus has been given credit for "discovering" America even though he only got as far as the Bahamas in 1492 and John Cabot landed in what is now Delaware in 1497. Slick Chris must have been sleeping with the right people to get credit for that. We've also conveniently managed to forget that American Indians had been here for thousands of years. How can someone "discover" something that's already been found and settled?

Getting back to Columbus, the Queen of England made a simple request that Chris go to France and get some French toast. The English weren't too bright back then and after what they've done to Northern Ireland, some would say they haven't learned too much since. Columbus was a freeloader and insisted that he needed two other ships to accompany him on this jaunt to France. The queen agreed because she was getting hungry and asked him to hurry. Columbus threw his supplies together and headed out of the harbor. He passed two small boats in the next two days but because both had women on them, he was too embarrassed to admit he didn't have a clue where he was, and he failed to ask them where France was located. So he kept sailing.

Within a few months he found France, about 4,000 miles west of where it was supposed to be and headed back to England. Like Lewis and Clark three hundred-plus years later, Columbus forgot what he had come for and left empty-handed. Much to the Queen's dismay, he came back with nothing but tales of "new land," so the Queen, eager to rid herself of this Columbus headache, sent him back to where he had just come from, this time with more ships and supplies.

If only we could do the same with our husbands. Send them out with ample supplies and not have to worry about them coming back for months. Instead, we have to go with them to make sure they find their destination and to make certain someone else's perfume and lipstick doesn't find its way into the back seat. Ever open up the glove compartment only to find panties that aren't yours? Just think back to the last time he went out in search of something alone. That's how they got there.

Maps are also too complicated for men to figure out. In defense of men, most women have difficulty in reading a map as well. Folding it is something no one can do right either and I won't get into that. My ex liked to drive around for an hour or so "looking at the scenery" and then pull to the side of the road and take out the map. "Just checking something," he'd say to me. We'd try driving from Portland, Oregon, to Reno, Nevada, and end up in Juneau, Alaska. All because I made the mistake of opening my mouth to say something at the U.S. border, like "do you want me to drive for a while?" Had I not said something to ruin his concentration, we would have made Reno in record time.

Auto racing is set up in such a way that men can have fun with their cars and not have to ask for directions. Just one continuous loop. The prizes men award each other for this brave feat can amount to millions of dollars and "the winners" are carried around on the shoulders of others as if they're heroes or something. Around and around they go, no chance of getting lost, except in the pits because they have to veer to the left and then merge to the right. That can be tricky for men, which is why they have so many accidents in the pits. Then again, maybe they're trying to fold the maps.

- 25 -
THE REMOTE CONTROL

What is it about the remote control that makes grown men act like little children? Walk into any room with a television on. If there's a man in there, he'll have the remote in one hand and a beer in the other. If there's more than one man, the others are constantly vying for their turn to hold the remote, but there's slim chance of them getting it. It's as if they were a pride of lions feasting over a kill: The first one there "owns" the carcass and the others have to fight for their fair share.

I suppose Freud would have had some sort of theory about how a man holds the remote. About how the remote control must be an extension of the penis, which is why it can't be shared or touched by others. How many men would get together with their buddies and watch a football game just so they could hold each other's penises? Maybe a group of men in San Francisco or a Republican congressional social event, but I can't see that happening anywhere else.

The next time you get a chance, watch a man with a remote in action. Don't let him know you're watching; be discreet. Maybe read a book in the same room and just feast your eyes on how he fondles, caresses and strokes the remote. He'll gently massage the sides of the device and delicately touch the buttons. Maybe he'll even lovingly tap the remote against his knee, as if he's trying to arouse it. You'd better be reading a funny book because you're bound to laugh out loud at his antics.

But don't try to change his behavior. All males have this trait firmly established in their genes. To prove this statement, watch a toddler or a group of young male children. The first thing the child wants to pick up is the remote. The male child knows it is his destiny to rule his tiny kingdom by having command of the remote. It takes precedence over the Golden Rule. ("He who has the gold makes the rules.")

Attitude goes along with controlling the remote. They all have this "attitude" that takes over. A perfectly intelligent man who's a practicing pacifist becomes aggressive with the remote. Volume? Don't bother asking. It must be perfect for him or else he'd change it. You have some sort of problem with your hearing because it's just fine with him. That brings up another point. The mute button must be mutilated. He already has volume control. You'd think that would be enough. But he has to wield control over that mute button like it's his own private possession, built especially for him.

You could hide the remote altogether so he can't watch television. Try that sometime. A man will search the house – turn it upside down – before manually turning on the television. It must be like trying to masturbate while his hand's asleep (talk about the ultimate rejection) – it just won't do. But now television manufacturers have invented what men have forever dreamed about: A remote locator. I have a television with this feature (it wasn't the reason I bought the set) and I've tried to get an understanding of the panic a man must go through. I hide the remote in my bedroom and manually turn on the television. The remote actually beeps for about thirty seconds until I can locate it.

A friend of mine recently hypothesized that humans will eventually evolve to the point where the males are born with a universal remote control imbedded in their chests, right above the sternum. That way they could master the remote at an early age while reclining in the La-Z-Boy watching a ball game. Maybe the remote will have burp recognition, something like speech recognition, that changes channels and volume depending on what type of burp is emitted. I wouldn't mind seeing that happen, but only if women grow a third hand that develops credit cards for fingers so we can get out of the house and do something while our husbands are content watching television all day.

- 26 -
PICKUP LINES AND HOW THEY SCORE

By using a scale of 0-100, we can see which lines men like to use and how positively or negatively women respond to the lines:

1. "I know we've just met but you might be interested to know I've recently swapped tongues with a cow."
Men's score: 80
Women's score: 5

2. "I know how to vacuum."
Men's score: 10
Women's score: 90

3. "When I was born the doctor said, 'That's one long umbilical cord.' It wasn't an umbilical cord."
Men's score: 95
Women's score: 35

4. "I'm a car mechanic. How about I show you the difference between a universal joint and a stick shift?"
Men's score: 60
Women's score: 15

5. "I used to be in the Air Force but they wouldn't let me fly because I prematurely ejected without warning...hey! Where are you going?"
Men's score: 0
Women's score: 0

6. "I really like talking to you because you've piqued my interest. The size of your...brain is impressive and I find your conversation titillating. Can I buy you some milk?"
Men's score: 75

Women's score: 10

7. "I'd have no problem with being a stay-at-home dad."
Men's score: 20
Women's score: 80

8. "I may be Jewish, but my nose isn't the only thing that's disproportionate in size."
Men's score: 50
Women's score: 20

9. "You look a lot like that woman in Fatal Attraction."
Men's score: 15
Woman's score: 60

10. "Here are two aspirins for your headache. What? You don't have a headache? Great! Let's go to bed!"
Men's score: 90
Women's score: 15

11. "The last time I went to the zoo, the elephants were jealous of me!"
Men's score: 80
Women's score: 25

12. "I know how to change a dirty diaper."
Men's score: 5
Women's score: 95

13. "If these were Roman times, my name would be cockus erectus."
Men's score: 65
Women's score: 15

14. (In church) "If I show you Gabriel's Horn, will you blow it?"

Men's score: 70
Women's score: 10

15. (In Iran) "I'd kill myself with a car bomb for you."
Men's score: 95
Women's score: 75

(For lesbians only)

1. "Your face or mine?"
First woman's score: 100
Second woman's score: 100

2. "You've been very open and honest with me. Can I be Frank with you?"
First woman's score: 100
Second woman's score: 100

(For gay men only)

1. "How would you like to eat, drink and be Mary?"
First man's score: 100
Second man's score: 100

2. "How about we explore each other's caves tonight?"
First man's score: 100
Second man's score: 100

- 27 -
PHONE SEX

There's nothing in the world that beats good phone sex and I have it about once a week. The standard wall phone doesn't work at all, so don't even bother. Phone sex is difficult enough without having to use a chair for balance and trying to keep your feet off the ceiling. I prefer the old fashioned phones, the kind that have the wide mouthpiece and the skinny part you listen with. Trouble is, I have a lot of people over to my home to visit and I never know who may have been using my phone before me, so protection is necessary. You should have seen the look on my pharmacist's face when I told him I needed a condom four inches wide and twelve inches long. He hasn't hit on me since.

Seriously though, phone sex between couples is natural and good, not to mention fun. If one partner travels around the country a lot, phone sex can fill the void left by that person being on the road. Maybe the husband is on a long business trip and is alone in his hotel room thinking about his wife. She's at home, thinking about him. He's a little horny and gives her a call. She's happy to hear from him and they both start in with a little phone sex. They strip each other naked, (unlike phone sex between strangers where there's just a lot of moaning and poor acting), feel each other up and maybe even climax at the same time (chances are that he'll beat her to the punch, though).

While phone sex between couples can be highly rewarding, my imaginary couple, Bill and Sue, once had phone sex that was more than erotic. A spontaneous phone call from Bill one night became an X-rated adventure. Here's how their conversation went:

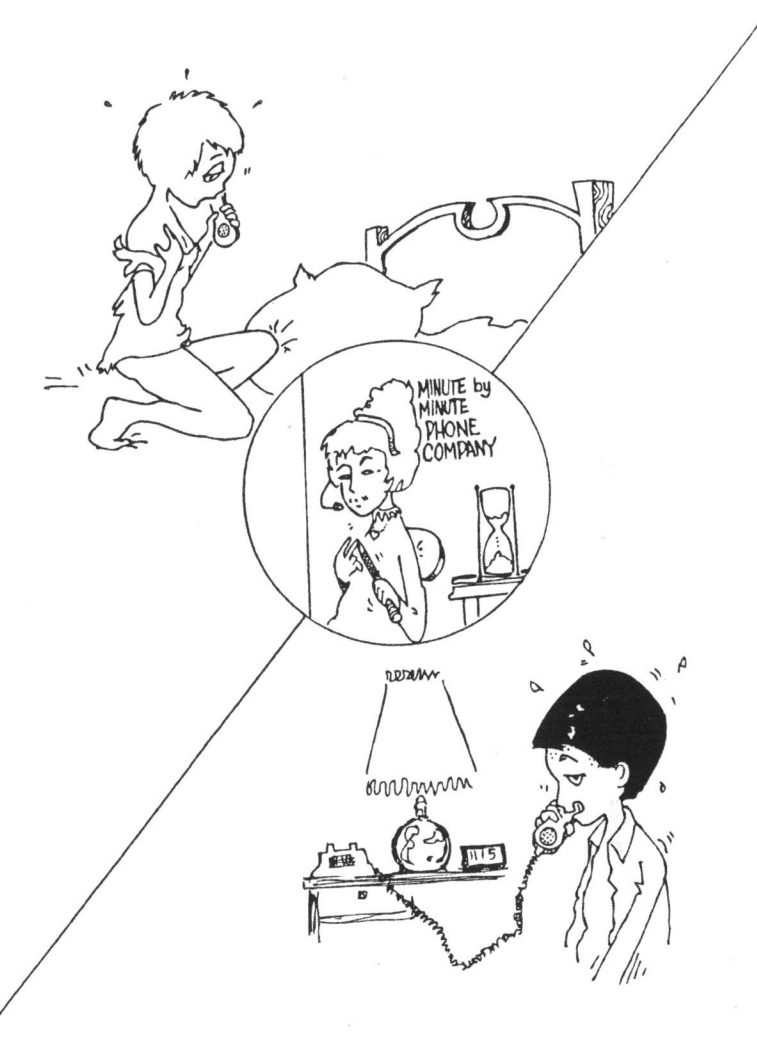

Bill: "Hi, honey. I was just thinking about you and wanted to give you a call."

Sue: "I'm glad you called. I was just thinking about you and getting hot."

Bill: "Getting hot, huh? Well maybe you'll get even hotter when I tell you I'm taking my shirt off."

Sue: "Oh, yeah, baby. You take that shirt off. You take it off!"

Bill: "What are you wearing?"

Sue: "My white negligee with the fuzzy ruffles."

Bill: "My hand is under that negligee, fondling your breasts. Am I good enough for you?"

Operator: "Sir, you have just one minute left on your calling card."

Sue: "Who the hell is that, Bill?"

Bill: "I don't know. Who is this?"

Operator: "This is the operator, sir. You have forty five seconds to use another card."

Sue: "Bill, is there another woman in that room with you?"

Bill: "No. She's on the phone."

Sue: "You have another woman with you and she's on another phone?"

Bill: "No, it's the operator. She's cutting in."

Operator: "You have just thirty seconds, sir."

Bill: "My other card's in my suitcase. Can't this wait?"

Sue: "Bill, I don't want this call to end."

Bill: "Neither do I."

Operator: "Only fifteen seconds, sir."

Bill: "Uh, operator?"

Operator: "Yes?"

Bill: "What are you wearing?"

Operator: "I thought you'd never ask. I've got on a short skirt and I'm not wearing any panties."

Bill: "Hey, Sue? You feel like a little three-way?"

Sue: "Anytime, anywhere."

Bill: "Okay. I've got two hands, ladies. You each get a hand; just tell me where you want it."

27443387R00086

Printed in Great Britain
by Amazon